On the Trail with

Your Canine Companion

On the Trail with
Your Canine Companion

Getting the Most Out of
Hiking and Camping with Your Dog

Cheryl S. Smith

**HOWELL
BOOK
HOUSE**
New York

Howell Book House

A Simon & Schuster Macmillan Company
1633 Broadway
New York, NY 10019

Library of Congress Cataloging-in-Publication Data available upon request.

ISBN: 0-87605-442-4

Manufactured in the United States of America

10 9 8 7 6 5 4 3 2 1

Design by Amy Peppler Adams—designLab, Seattle

To all the land managers open-minded enough to allow dogs to walk their trails, and all the dog owners responsible enough to encourage continued acceptance.

Contents

Contents

Acknowledgments

I would like to thank veterinarian Dennis Wilcox of Angeles Clinic for Animals, Mandy Book of Oz Training, and Judy Winthrop for their thoughtful comments on the manuscript. They made many improvements. Any problems remain the responsibility of the author. Also, thanks to Dominique De Vito at Howell Book House, who provided enthusiasm and common sense along the way. For additional photography, I am indebted to Kim Peterson, R. Randal Son, Tim and Wendy Paradis, and Kent and Donna Dannen for the excellent cover. Mostly, I thank Sundance, Spirit, Serling, Starsky, Harry-O and Diamond, who always make a trail or a camp more enjoyable.

Your Canine Companion

Introduction

When we had set out, the sky was blue and clear. Now the clouds were so thick and low that only the next five feet of trail were visible. Even without visual reference, I knew the turns to take to backtrack, and, failing that, I could rely on the compass I carried. But I had always wondered whether in an emergency my dog would be of any help. Now seemed like a good time to conduct a test.

I stopped at a three-trail junction and tried to look and sound seriously distressed (fooling a dog about your emotional state is no easy task). "Oh no, Sundance, we're lost! Which way do we go?"

Not understanding that particular bit of English, my Keeshond companion just looked at me and waved her tail once to let me know she was listening. Now I used the phrase I knew would get results if any were going to be gotten: "Where's the car?"

Sundance, like most dogs allowed to accompany their humans on trips, viewed the car as an object of reverence only slightly less important than her food bowl. It took us to wonderful places, and it was a place in which she could wait and be sure of my speedy return. If she knew where the car was and accepted that I needed help in finding it, she would lead me to it.

The author's dog Serling on the trail with a hiking companion and her dog Diamond.

She gave me a searching look. I doubt that she really believed we were lost, but she played along. After a few sniffs, she set off down the correct trail. I didn't have to ask her again. At some junctions, she stopped and carefully checked the choices before proceeding; others she just breezed on through (I would guess this depended on wind direction). Though we had passed or been passed by at least a dozen other hikers, some with their own dogs, Sundance had no trouble at all leading us directly back to the pull-out where the car was parked.

I have never had to use this backtracking ability (my only close call came in a fogged-in volcanic crater where I suffered altitude sickness, but of course I couldn't bring my dog with me to Hawaii), but it is nice to know it's there.

Most of the pleasures of camping and hiking with dogs are less dramatic than wilderness rescue. Dogs are simply fine trail and fireside companions. They never complain that you burned the hamburgers or forgot the bug spray or missed the turn on the lake loop trail. They're happy to be with you, whether it's lounging around in camp or pushing on for another mile.

But bringing your dog along isn't simply a matter of leaving some space in the car and throwing the dog bowl on top of the pile. Just as you plan for your comfort and safety, you need to prepare for your dog's. The first chapter of this book will discuss pretrip preparations. Some are quite a bit "pre," but it's never too early to start.

Chapter 2 discusses packing. If you're one of those camping families that bring along three carloads of goods in one bulging car, adding even the few things your dog will require could prove a challenge. Remember that all members of the expedition require a certain amount of space to be happy while traveling—that includes the dog. Chapter 3 goes over other car considerations.

Most campers do at least some hiking, and some people don't camp but hike for miles and miles. Chapters 4 and 5 examine the hazards and the pleasures of the trail. The hazards can seem a bit overwhelming, but many of them apply whether you are accompanied by a dog or not. Don't let them discourage you from bringing Bowser along. The special pleasures can be experienced only in the company of a dog.

Chapter 6 looks at the campground and how a canine fits in. The rules have changed considerably since I first started bringing dogs along, so even if you and a canine camped in the past, you can probably learn something new here.

Chapter 7 takes a quick look at ways your dog can really pull his or her weight. If you are seriously interested in sledding, dog packing or other dog-powered activities, there are other books that concentrate specifically on those subjects to help get you started. A listing of some is included in Appendix B.

Responsibility is discussed in chapter 8. This is a subject especially dear to my heart, because only by constantly demonstrating conscientious behavior can we keep the wild places open to us and our dogs. In a world of ever-increasing regulation, you are a representative of a group, whether you like it or not. One or two thoughtless travelers can jeopardize the rights of an entire class of outdoor enthusiasts, whether they are mountain bikers, equestrians or dog owners. Chapter 8 touches on how your efforts might even open up areas that have excluded dogs in the past.

In Appendix A you will find a list of addresses and phone numbers for state and national parks departments, campground organizations and tourist bureaus. In general, your dog will be welcome in most campgrounds, but will probably be banned from trails in national parks. National forests are generally less restrictive, and Bureau of Land Management properties are usually the most welcoming toward dogs. State parks vary widely. It is best to check beforehand rather than find yourself miles from any boarding facility, with your plans ruined because your dog is not allowed on that backpacking expedition you mapped out.

Appendix B offers books that may prove helpful, organizations that may interest you, and other items of potential interest.

Be aware that how you and your dog are viewed can often have an impact on whether you are allowed to stay somewhere. Sundance was so obviously a princess among dogs, with better manners than many people, that she was welcomed at lodgings from coast to coast. Campgrounds were never a problem. I doubt that my two Retriever mixes would receive the same welcome. Though well-trained, they are big and exuberant and often look like they are cooking up some sort of devilry (and they often are).

I hope this book will help you and your dog have many rewarding expeditions together. If you have any suggestions for future editions, or any hiking or camping anecdotes you would like to pass along, please write to me care of the publisher. It's always nice to hear from others who share the camping experience with their dogs. But it's even nicer to be out on the trail!

Cheryl S. Smith
with Sundance, Spirit and Serling
Port Angeles, Washington

CHAPTER 1

Preparing for Your Adventures

As I mentioned in the introduction, preparation can occur quite a long time before an actual trip. In fact, socializing your puppy from the age of six or eight weeks is the start of preparing him to deal with all sorts of events throughout his life. A puppy who learns to accept different situations, strange people and other animals becomes a dog eager for new experiences, able to adjust to unique circumstances.

If your dog is no longer a puppy and he hasn't been exposed to much of the world, don't despair: Old dogs can indeed be taught new tricks; it just takes longer.

The Keeshond I already mentioned (Sundance) started traveling with me almost from the day we came together. She accompanied me in cars, on foot and on horseback (me, not the dog!). She was always a perfect traveling companion, with better manners than many people I've known. I can take no credit for her excellence—she came that way.

The youngest of my canine companions (Serling) is quite another story. He came bent on destruction and convinced that all other animals on earth were meant to be either chased or retrieved. If he couldn't catch them, he'd bark at them ad infinitum. He was carsick, chewed whatever was available whenever left alone, and once

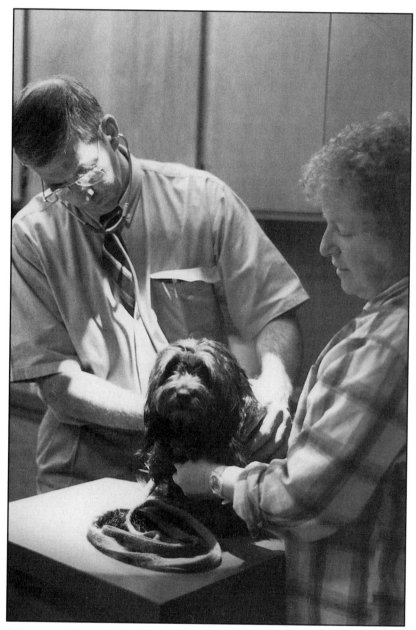

Before you hit the trail, make sure your dog is in good health by taking her for a thorough physical examination.

jumped out of the window of a moving car. I take as much credit as possible for the fact that he is now an acceptable fellow traveler, though still a bit noisy at times.

It took work to change Serling from a constant annoyance to a constant companion. It was worth every minute, not just for traveling, but for everyday living.

Whether your dog is a shining example like Sundance or a test case like Serling, traveling together can work.

How Fit Is Your Dog?

One important prerequisite to any new activity is a health checkup. We've all heard the admonition, "consult your physician before beginning an exercise program." This is doubly true for your dog. Not only will a layabout Lab or couch potato Cocker be ill-prepared for a sudden expedition of a mile or more, they will try so hard to please you that they may push themselves beyond their limits. To be sure that your trip is a safe and happy one for all involved, make an appointment with your veterinarian to have your dog's health checked.

The actual details of a health examination may vary from one veterinarian to another. In general, the exam will include the following:

- Listening to the heart for any murmurs or arrhythmia

- Checking that the lungs sound clear

- Taking a temperature

- Examining eyes for any vision problems or abnormal discharge

- Checking ears for any foreign bodies or signs of infection

- Looking in the mouth for swollen gums, cracked teeth or other problems

- Feeling the abdomen for any tenderness or unusual masses

- Watching the dog's movement for balance, good reach and drive

- Manipulating each leg to check for normal range of motion

- Examining the pads of the feet for cuts, thin spots or excess hair

- Checking the length of toenails

- Weighing the dog

For older or overweight dogs, your veterinarian may want to check the blood chemistry or ask you to exercise the dog for some time, then check heart and breathing rates again.

If your dog is elderly and somewhat frail, your vet may suggest that it would be kinder to leave him home with a sitter or use a good boarding kennel. You know your dog better than anyone else, but don't let your heart rule your mind. If the senior canine no longer wants to be outside on frosty mornings for any longer than necessary, a cold-weather camping trip would not be a good idea. But if your dog refuses to eat whenever business takes you away overnight, a week's vacation without him could prove disastrous. You must make the decision.

The health check is also the time to see that all vaccinations are current and to discuss any additional procedures that may be necessary, such as being vaccinated for Lyme disease or checked for heartworm. Don't hesitate to ask questions about any specific conditions you may expect to encounter.

If your dog is out of condition but otherwise healthy, read the section in this chapter on conditioning, and discuss with your veterinarian a safe exercise program for your dog.

Your Canine Good Citizen certificate may come in handy should you need to convince someone of your dog's good manners.

Papers You'll Need

While you are having a health check done on your dog, ask your veterinarian for a health certificate for your dog. Some campgrounds will require that you show this document before checking in. It is also necessary in border crossings. The certificate simply states that your dog is not obviously suffering from any communicable diseases and that vaccinations are current.

Also ask your vet to write out a list of any medications your dog takes regularly, with suitable substitutions if possible. You should, of course, take a supply of the medicines with you, but things happen—they may be lost, or in an emergency the veterinarian seeing your dog may need to know all those long tongue-twister names. That old Boy Scout slogan "Be prepared" is especially apropos in the wilderness.

You should have a rabies certificate or a dog license stating that the dog's rabies vaccine is current for the period covered by the license.

Without these documents, you risk being turned away from your chosen campground. And in some areas, that may be the *only* campground.

Other papers that may prove useful are copies of any obedience certificates your dog has earned and the Canine Good Citizen test certificate. These could swing the verdict in your favor if you are trying to talk your way into some lodgings that are doubtful about accepting your dog.

Conditioning Your Dog

Roadwork is one of the best ways to condition your dog. It involves running or bicycling with your dog in tow, starting slow but building up distance and endurance. But it's a lot of work for both of you, and if you're lucky enough to have a natural retriever and an area where your dog can be off-leash, hitting a tennis ball for the dog to retrieve can exercise the dog while you expend relatively little energy. Swimming is a truly excellent conditioning activity as well.

If your exercise program will involve roadwork and your dog will need some work to get fit, remember that *moderation* is the watchword. Your dog's pads will need a chance to toughen up, especially if your exercise is on pavement. And you don't want to work the dog to exhaustion. For a dog that is truly out of condition, maybe a slow jog to the end of the block and back is enough to start. Every week or so, add a little more distance.

For dogs that are already in decent shape—not severely overweight and accustomed to regular (even if somewhat mild) exercise—you should go fast enough to force the dog into a trot. If you are not yourself a jogger, or if you have a large breed with a

Swimming is great exercise for your dog.

stride considerably longer than your own, reaching a speed to break your dog into a trot may be beyond *your* abilities. In such a case, you may want to consider bicycling.

There are several devices designed to attach a dog to a bicycle so that dog and rider are safe. They allow the dog enough room to move without getting caught in the wheels and without being able to pull you off balance. Even with them, it is a good idea to get your dog used to trotting alongside the bike before venturing into any traffic areas. My veterinarian has treated some nasty crashes, with damage to both participants, which were a result of diverging ideas on direction on the parts of dog and rider. Also, since bicycling will make it easier for you to go farther and faster, be doubly attentive for any signs that your dog is tiring. Again, start with short distances and gradually work up to approximately two miles.

If there's any sort of swimming hole nearby that you and your dog can use, by all means take advantage of it. Swimming is especially beneficial for older dogs or dogs recovering from surgery. It has excellent cardiovascular benefits without the stress to joints experienced in roadwork. Again, this is easier with Retrievers, as they will fetch thrown sticks or tennis balls or bumpers. With other dogs, you may have to do some swimming yourself!

Identification

Quick, which of your dog's feet has that distinctive white toe? Is it the left or right ear that flops over while the other stands up? How big and what color is that spot on his left side? It's amazing how hard it can be to describe the dog you feed and pet every day.

At home, of course, you can just turn your head and look at that floppy ear or that one white toe. But if disaster struck and your dog disappeared in a strange place, could you be sure to give an accurate, detailed description?

I can hear you protesting that you would never be so careless as to lose your dog in the wilderness. But it has happened to other people who felt exactly the same way, and it could happen to you, too. A deer bounding away up the trail might elicit an irresistible chase response. Or a thunderstorm could freak out your usually placid pet. It is precisely such unexpected events that can result in a lost dog.

Two friends of mine were attending an obedience trial at a fairgrounds over the Fourth of July weekend. They knew one of their dogs, Breeze, was easily rattled by noise, and they weren't taking any chances—or so they thought. Both dogs did well, and my friends were called to accept their awards near the end of day. The dogs were in their familiar exercise pen, and it was no noisier than the usual dog show—everything seemed fine. But while the awards were being presented, the fireworks crew set off a few preliminary blasts to check their equipment. When my friends hurried back to their setup, the exercise pen was knocked down and Breeze was gone.

The situation still didn't seem that bad: The fairgrounds were fenced, and there were lots of people around. They informed the show secretary of the missing dog and set out searching.

Everyone at the show knew what a Belgian Tervuren looked like, because they spent a lot of time around many different breeds. Their sighting reports were reliable. Breeze was seen first at one end of the fairgrounds, then at the other, then slipping out a gate. She was running wild, crazed with fear.

It was after dark and several miles down a back road when Breeze was finally located and coaxed into her familiar car. The story had a happy ending, but everyone involved was shaken.

So follow the "prepare for the worst and it won't happen" axiom. Before leaving home, write out a detailed description of your dog and collect some clear photographs. They will prove invaluable if you have to search for your pet. An identification tag is another essential. I hope that your dog wears one on a regular basis. But the usual information—your home address and phone number—will not be very useful if you are all away on vacation. Even if you have a housesitter, can you be sure he or she will be there to answer the phone in an emergency? And will someone know how to contact you quickly? Better to take care of it yourself.

There are several choices of temporary identification for your dog. The best option if you will be changing locations several times is a small canister or pouch that attaches to the collar. The barrel or pocket opens, and inside is a piece of paper on which you can write your up-to-date contact information. There are also temporary tags made of heavy-stock paper, which hang off

the collar the same as a permanent metal tag. Be sure to use indelible ink when marking these tags, or a dog lost in the rain may lose his identification as well. Either of these arrangements allow you to change the address and phone number as you change your campground. You will, of course, have to remember to make this change at each appropriate time, and it may not work well if you are driving long distances between campgrounds and your dog is lost at some transition point. But you want every possible means of finding your dog should he become lost, and an ID tag is a definite plus.

Another option is a tattoo. Pet supply stores and breed or obedience clubs often offer tattooing clinics once or twice a year. The numbers used may be your dog's AKC registration number, your driver's license number, or your social security number (note that the government will definitely *not* release a person's name if given a social security number). Tattoos are now most often placed on the inside of the dog's thigh.

Dogs react differently to the tattooing process. Some lie quietly; some even wag their tails, happy with the attention. Some appear to be tickled by the vibration. And a few scream as if they were being dismembered, even before the tattooer makes contact. No matter how a dog reacts, the procedure is quickly finished. The tattooers insist it doesn't hurt, but given varying pain thresholds, there is no way to know whether it does for any particular animal. You can take heart in the knowledge that it is a useful safety precaution and needs to be done only once in most cases.

Whatever number you choose to tattoo your dog with, it will not be of much use unless it is registered with one of the national organizations. Three of these groups are the National Dog Registry, Tattoo-a-Pet, and I.D. Pet (see Appendix B for addresses and phone numbers). The tattooer will often be working with one of these groups and will charge for registering your dog as part of the tattooing fee.

A tattoo is an excellent pet-theft deterrent. But its value in recovering a lost pet is questionable. The person who finds the dog has first to look for a tattoo, then be aware of the tattoo organization and know how to contact them. Some owners solve this problem by using an ID tag with the registry's phone number, or having the phone number tattooed beneath the registration number. This combination should prove effective, as long as the tattoo is noticed.

There are also a few companies that provide an answering service for dogs that are lost but not tattooed. They use 800-numbers (which you would presumably include on your dog's ID tag) that are answered twenty-four hours a day, seven days a week. Their addresses and phone numbers are also listed in Appendix B. (Note that your dog has to be registered with the company prior to being lost.)

One final form of ID is the relatively new electronic chip. This rice-sized pellet encoded with a digital number is implanted in your dog at the base of the neck, between the shoulder blades. It can be read with a scanner, and the information links the dog to you. The value of this device while traveling is still questionable. Most people wouldn't think to have a lost dog scanned. The local animal shelter or veterinarian may have a scanner, but it might not be the right brand (there are four different systems currently on the market, some cross-compatible and some not). Most chips carry an ID code identifying the system used so that those scanning the chip can contact the correct organization. The AKC has also started the "Companion Animal Recovery" program, registering microchipped dogs and providing a twenty-four-hour phone line for reporting lost or found dogs. (See appendix B for the program's address and phone number.)

If a chip registry is contacted, they will attempt to contact you directly rather than releasing your name to the person calling. So if your dog has a microchip and gets lost while traveling, call the registry at once and let them know where they can reach you in case someone calls them. As chips increase in popularity, they will undoubtedly become more uniform and easier to trace to the owner.

Training

This is indeed pretrip preparation—maybe very much "pre," depending on your relationship with your dog.

Would your dog come to you in almost any situation? If not, you should train your dog to come reliably.

Basic training should be part of every dog's life. Though it is easier with puppies, it is effective with dogs of any age. If you have neglected your dog's education to this point, an impending trip is an excellent reason to correct this oversight.

If you were on the trail and your leash broke or your dog slipped his collar, could you call him to you? Not without training. A well-conditioned recall could mean the difference between a happy vacation and one spent desperately seeking Suzie the Beagle.

Another extremely useful result of training is the ability to stop a dog in place, whether it be to sit, down or simply stop and wait.

There are all sorts of options for dog-training—groups, private, or even on your own via books or videos. If you have not trained a dog before, group classes are a good choice. You will not only receive instruction, you will see others struggling to master this new skill. Make no mistake—*you* are going to school every bit as much as your dog. You must learn how to communicate first and then enforce your wishes to your non-English-speaking companion.

Yes, training involves work on your part. It is work that every dog owner should do. Not only will it make your dog a better companion, it will strengthen the bond between you, and it may even give you some tips on how to cope with spouses, bosses and children. You will better understand your canine and have a better idea of how to deal with any problems that may arise.

In many areas, there are now classes focusing on the Canine Good Citizen test (CGC). Some even offer the test as graduation. It is a low-key exam, checking for basic good manners such as walking on a leash without pulling and performing the sit and down on command. It even includes a recall so you won't neglect this vital exercise in your training.

A Canine Good Citizen certificate is starting to provide some perks to dogs and their owners. In the county where I reside, a CGC lowers your dog-license fee. In other places, it allows you off-leash privileges. It can even serve as a device to stop the spread of anti-dog legislation. It's possible that campgrounds may start to waive the

17

How to Choose a Dog Trainer

It's important to find someone you're comfortable with to train your dog. Here are the ten most important things to ask about and look for:

1. How many years has the person been training dogs?

2. What type of training does the person offer? Is it basic obedience geared toward obedience trial competition, basic obedience for the pet owner, problem-solving training, or specialized training?

3. Does the trainer provide group classes, private sessions or both? If groups, how many students are there in a class? how long are the classes? and if the classes are large, is there an assistant? If private, how long and how often are the sessions?

4. How much do classes cost? How much are private sessions?

5. How much experience has the trainer had with your breed (or breed type)? How does he or she feel about your breed?

6. What's the trainer's background? How did he or she learn to train and get experience in training?

7. What training clubs or organizations (if any) does the trainer belong to?

8. What training equipment does the trainer use, and is the equipment included in the cost of the training?

9. Can you come and observe a class or session? It's important to see how the trainer relates to the students—humans and dogs—and vice versa. Look at how the class or trainee is managed, how the dogs are responding, what the general mood is, how much attention students are getting, and so on.

> 10. Can the trainer give you references—a veterinarian or people whose dogs have gone through his or her classes?
>
> The Association of Pet Dog Trainers (APDT), a national organization, can refer you to a trainer in your area. Contact APDT at P.O. Box 3734, Salinas, CA 93912; (408) 663-9257. You can also ask for recommendations from your veterinarian, friends or a humane organization in your area.

additional fee for dogs with a CGC, or even require the CGC for a dog to be admitted. The CGC is a worthwhile and achievable goal. For more information about it, contact the American Kennel Club at the address listed in Appendix B.

Spend some time choosing an obedience instructor. There are different training theories in use right now, and you should practice one that appeals to you. If you are soft-hearted and think jerking on a choke chain is inhumane, the traditional method will probably not suit you. If you believe you have to be the alpha pack leader and take control, positive food-reward training may strike you as namby-pamby. Watch a prospective instructor in action, and decide whether his or her methods are something you can use every day. Also ask whether your instructor has had experience with your breed or type of dog. Observe a class in session, and afterward, when the instructor is not busy, you may ask questions about any special concerns you have.

You should expect a basic training class to teach you how to teach your dog such necessary behavior as coming when called, sitting and lying down on command, staying in one place until told it's alright to move, and walking on a leash or, more formally, heeling. Some classes may also include playtime (socialization to other dogs), stand on command, watch (focusing your dog's attention on you), leave it (not to touch some object, person or dog), and a variety of other commands.

Instructors should keep things under control at all times—even if a roomful of puppies are off-leash having playtime—and be on

Some places specify that dogs should be kept on-leash. Follow the rules!

the lookout for handlers having problems. You should not expect a group class to stand around while you seek advice on some unique problem of your own, but you should get help with any activities the class is expected to master.

Keep in mind that basic training will not solve all the problems you might encounter in the campground. Barking is a big one not always addressed in regular classes. And it is a sin that can get you summarily ejected from a campground.

Many puppy classes include teaching dogs to "quiet" or "shush" as part of their normal training. Other classes will work on any special problems of their participants. Ask your trainer for help before or after class sessions.

If you are on your own with this one, you can use a trick many professionals know: To get rid of or control a behavior, first put it on command. In other words, if you need to tell your dog when to *stop* barking, first teach him to *start* barking when you say. Anticipate a situation that will get your dog barking; then, while he's at it, give a command to "speak" or "alert" (or whatever word you choose). Allow him a few lusty barks, then tell him "Good boy, now 'quiet' or 'hush' (or whatever)." Toss him a cookie (which automatically gives you a moment of silence), and praise him for being quiet. Try to remove the stimulus that set off the barking so that he won't start again.

Remember that no new skill is learned overnight, and keep working at it. Good manners will be appreciated not only in camp but every day at home. If you have some serious problems outside the range of normal group classes, talk to an instructor about private training.

Other problems are more easily solved. Your dog can't chase animals if he's on a leash. Chasing after deer or cattle (which you will often encounter grazing on public land) is an offense punishable by death—a dog caught in the act can be shot! Do not risk such consequences, or the more likely scenario that your dog may fight with and be bitten by a raccoon (a rabies carrier in many parts of the

United States). Or even that he will simply run off after something and not come back.

Some areas specify that dogs be kept on-leash. Others use wording such as "under control at all times." Do not think your dog will be "under control" off-leash unless you have done some serious work with him. And remember that you might be sharing a trail with horses, mountain bikers, pack mules or llamas. Your dog must not bother any of these, or other hikers and dogs. This level of control is not easily achieved. And even with control, unexpected things can happen.

My middle dog, Spirit, was always good about staying near me and ignoring other animals. Only around waterfowl would I keep a tight grip on her, as she just knew she was supposed to bring those things to me. But the river we were walking along one day didn't seem to be home to ducks or waterbirds of any kind, so Spirit was off-leash. I was calling her back to me every so often, just to be sure I had control, because the river was running pretty swiftly and I didn't want her getting into any trouble. She was showing good sense, staying in the shallows and keeping an eye on my whereabouts. She climbed onto a rock a little ways into the river and stood on top scouting her territory. She made a very pretty picture up there, until a stick floated by in the rushing current on the other side of the rock. In a flash, Spirit, the consummate Retriever, had launched herself off the rock into the river and was being swept downstream. It didn't matter how much I called now, she couldn't come to me even if she wanted to. I ran along the bank, trying to keep up with her rapid progress. She was soon far beyond me.

It took some time, but we met up maybe a quarter of a mile farther along, me still hurrying downstream, she walking back to me, carrying that stick.

I should have known better. But at least I got to learn my lesson with no harm to person or dog.

Emergencies

As you drive through towns and cities, you may notice that there are signs directing you to the local hospital. There are no such signs for veterinarians. I hope that you will have no need for emergency services of any kind, but things do happen. Knowing the location of the nearest vet can offer peace of mind, or it can prove to be life-saving information.

The chamber of commerce of the town nearest your camping site should be able to provide the name, address and phone number of a local veterinarian. Or your own veterinarian may have resource books that can provide this information for the United States, Canada and Mexico.

In areas where there are no twenty-four-hour emergency clinics, vets can often be reached for emergencies at all hours of the day or night. Common sense and, I hope, the information in this book should help prevent a need for such services.

But . . .

. . . Jumping into the car on the first day of a ten-day trip, Sundance caught a toe on some piece of the door frame and tore a nail.

. . . After a lovely run in the first of several planned visits to off-leash areas, Harry-O began sneezing violently and repeatedly. Was this a grass allergy (probably not—dogs get itchy skin rather than sneezing fits as their usual allergic response, but I didn't know that then) or a foxtail in her nose? Just as we finally located a veterinarian along the road, she stopped and didn't sneeze again the entire trip.

So you never know. Prelocating veterinarians all along your travel route is probably not something you want to do, but at least having a name and phone number for an area where you'll be staying is not a waste of time.

What to Do if Your Dog Goes into Shock or Chokes

Even if you take every precaution for safety, accidents can happen—especially when you're hiking, camping or backpacking. This is true for your dog as well as yourself. Knowing how to handle an emergency situation can mean the difference between life and death.

Cardiopulmonary resuscitation (CPR) is a technique you can't afford not to know how to do. You can use it on people and animals—it's as easy as A (Airway), B (Breathing), C (Circulation).

CPR must be performed in a specific order to be effective. Here are the steps you must follow:

1. Assess your dog's condition. Is he in shock? Signs to look for are lethargy, pale gums, shallow breathing and cool paws. If he's up at all, your dog will appear very disoriented. Keep him as quiet as possible.

2. Get help. If you're with a friend, send that person to call for a veterinarian (you should have the number of a local vet in your emergency kit). If you're by yourself, do the best you can to stabilize your dog, then get to the veterinarian as soon as possible.

3. Check your dog's Airway for any obstructions. It helps to extend the neck and pull the tongue forward.

4. Check your dog's Breathing. If his throat appears clear but he's not breathing, begin mouth-to-muzzle artificial respiration. The best way to get the most air in is to cup your hands around his closed muzzle, then blow gently into the nostrils. See whether his chest is rising and falling with the breaths. Do this three times.

5. Check your dog's Circulation. Place him on his right side. Feel for the heartbeat by pressing two fingers on the chest, just below the elbow. That's where you'll get the strongest

pulse. If his heart's beating but your dog is not breathing, keep giving him artificial respiration, counting eight to ten breaths per minute, until he's breathing on his own. If you don't feel a heartbeat and your dog's not breathing, begin CPR.

6. Keep your dog on his right side and make sure he's on a hard surface. Using the heel of your hand, put it against your dog's chest, just below the elbow (use two hands for dogs over forty-five pounds.) Press down rapidly and firmly six times, allowing a couple of seconds between each push. After six pushes, give three mouth-to-muzzle breaths as described above. Repeat this cycle, checking every minute or two for breathing and heartbeat. Keep this up for five to ten minutes, then get to a veterinarian, continuing mouth-to-muzzle respiration and/or CPR en route, if possible.

Choking

If you notice your dog suddenly salivating excessively, breathing with difficulty, pawing at her mouth or having trouble eating or drinking, she may have something stuck in her throat. What should you do?

1. See whether her airway is clogged with something.

2. If it is, strike your dog's chest; her coughing may be able to dislodge the object. Repeat this four times.

3. If she's still struggling for breath, you'll need to give her the Heimlich maneuver, an abdominal thrust. Stand her on all fours, kneel or stand behind her, and with an open hand on either side of her, grasp her just past her rib cage. Squeeze with both hands, pressing upward. Do this four times. The force of the thrusts should expel the object.

4. Open her mouth to see whether she has coughed up the object. Extend her neck and pull her tongue forward if you can. If there's something there, remove it. If need be, give

your dog mouth-to-muzzle respiration to help her breath normally.

5. Alternate the chest strikes with the abdominal thrusts and artificial respiration until she coughs up the object. If your dog loses consciousness, get her to a veterinarian as soon as possible. Continue the sequence en route, if possible.

If you're confused about how to perform any of these procedures, discuss them with your veterinarian.

Regulations

Many, many parks permit dogs in campgrounds but ban them from all trails. Others open only specified trails. To avoid disappointment, it's a good idea to check on regulations while you are planning your trip. There are wilderness areas that will welcome you and your dog for a walk; it just takes some effort to find them.

Since regulations change unexpectedly, any specific information I might give in this book could quickly become outdated. Use the addresses and phone numbers in the appendix to contact park departments and get up-to-date information. Also contact the individual parks or wilderness areas you will be visiting. The sites themselves will sometimes provide information that conflicts with what the governing organization says. For example, a call to the California Department of Parks and Recreation will probably net you the warning that dogs are not allowed on any trails in state parks. But a talk with the rangers at Samuel P. Taylor State Park in Marin will result in the more welcome news that dogs are permitted on fire roads and their lovely bike path along the river. Many other such discrepancies undoubtedly exist.

If you're willing to be flexible, you can explore the opportunities when you arrive at each site. If not, invest in some phone calls and know what restrictions await you.

So that you're not disappointed when you arrive, check in advance to make sure your destination allows dogs.

Why Bother?

I'm sure there's someone out there who has read this far, snorted, and said "I'm planning a vacation because I need a break! What do I need with all this extra work?" Well, much of it really has nothing to do with your trip. Your dog should have current vaccinations, some form of permanent identification, and basic obedience training, whether you ever go camping or not. As to the rest, you make plans for your own comfort and safety, don't you?

If you are not willing to invest the pretrip time and effort needed to include your dog safely, you are not likely to show the necessary flexibility on the trip itself. You must be prepared to adjust activities to accommodate the dog when unexpected problems arise. The dog has to be a full member of the expedition, entitled to as much consideration as anyone else.

For most of you, I'm sure that your dog is a valued companion and you enjoy your time together however it is spent.

CHAPTER 2

Packing

Camping can involve anything from staying in a recreational vehicle, with all the luxuries of home, to roughing it with only what you can carry on your back. What you pack for yourself will be quite different for these extremes. But packing for your dog, except for the last one or two items, stays pretty much the same.

What to Pack

You will generally need to bring the following:

- The paperwork mentioned in chapter 1 (health certificate, rabies vaccination certificate, dog license)

- A spare collar and leash

- Food and water bowls

- The dog's usual food (unless it will be available where you are traveling)

- Water from home

The car is packed and ready to go, complete with dogs and dog equipment!

- Any medications your dog normally takes

- Flea/tick powder or spray

- Comb or brush, tweezers, scissors

- Plastic bags

- Old towels

- Coat or sweater for dog

- First-aid kit

- Toys and/or chews

- Blanket/kennel mat/sleeping bag

- Crate, exercise pen, tie-out, some form of restraint

Chapter 1 already discussed why you need the health certificate and other paperwork. The spare leash and collar are equally indispensable. There's not likely to be a convenient pet supply store in the Goat Rocks Wilderness Area. In a pinch, a length of decent nonscratchy rope will do. Just be sure you have some form of backup restraint.

Why? Picture this. You've had a long morning's hike to a secluded lake. There's no one else around, you've looked the place over, and decided it's safe to let your dog off leash. She cavorts along the lake edge for a while, then decides to go for a swim. You enjoy watching her. For a second, her head bobs under and you get up, afraid she might be caught on something, but she's swimming again and everything appears to be fine. When she returns to shore, she isn't wearing a collar. It's out in that lake on whatever snagged her momentarily. And camp is ten miles back through cattle-grazing grounds.

You can teach your dogs to drink out of water bottles; they're easy to carry on hikes.

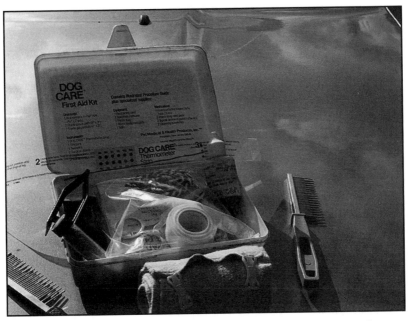

You can assemble your own canine first-aid kit or buy one that's already prepared. In either case, first-aid supplies are essential.

This did indeed happen. Fortunately the dog's owner still had a leash, which he used as a makeshift slip collar and leash combination, and they got back to camp safely.

The food and water bowls you pack do not have to be your dog's usual ones if they are too bulky. In fact, there are special collapsible bowls for travel. One consists of progressively larger circles of rigid plastic that pull up to create a bowl and push down to nest inside one another (the same as the plastic "travel glasses" that were once popular). There is also a bowl of nonrigid plastic that rolls up to the size of a tube of lipstick. And there is a pet canteen, useful both in camp and on the trail. Or you can just choose two regular bowls so that one fits inside the other. Or use a dog bowl for food and share a human-type water bottle, if you have taught your dog to drink this way.

For chilly mornings and evenings, you may want to have a T-shirt or sweater for your dog.

How much food you need to bring depends on where you will be camping. If your stay will be at Heart of the Hills in Olympic National Park in Washington state, you are just up the mountains from the town of Port Angeles and several pet shops. But if you're spending a few days hoping to catch the desert bloom in Mojave National Scenic Area in California, it's a long drive to a small town. Plan accordingly. No matter where your travels are taking you, bring food for at least the first few days—you aren't going to want to run around looking for dog food when you've just arrived.

Opinions differ on how much water you should carry from home. I always thought it strange that dog-care books advised you to bring water from home for your dog but that human travelers were not directed to take the same precautions (unless they were going to Mexico or other exotic locations with uncertain water supplies). Of course you should have water for your dog in the car, but once you arrive at a campground, assuming it has potable water, why can you drink it while your dog can't?

I checked with some veterinarians on this issue. They advised that for dogs with sensitive stomachs, "foreign" water can cause digestive upset. I suspect that the same is true for people. The bottom line seems to be that unless you know your dog's innards are easily upset, if you're planning on drinking the water, your dog can, too.

If your dog is on medication of any kind, be sure to bring an adequate supply.

Camping and hiking mean contact with the wild. And that means fleas and ticks. A good flea and tick powder or spray is essential equipment. A friend who camps regularly with a Tibetan Terrier mix and a Boxer reports that applying a good dusting of flea powder before venturing into the wilderness has always worked well for her. No ticks at all and no noticeable flea infestation. This is an important precaution, as both fleas and ticks carry potentially deadly diseases that can affect both dogs and humans. In fact, I've known some hikers who dust down their dogs and then their own ankles before setting off on the trail.

Basic grooming tools are also essential. If, despite your best efforts, ticks do attach themselves, they should be removed as soon as possible. Tweezers will prove invaluable for this, as well as for splinter removal. A comb or brush and pair of scissors (even the small scissors of a Swiss army knife) can all be valuable in removing foxtails and the many other spiny, sticky weeds you may encounter.

Anyone venturing very far outside the city limits should pack a basic first-aid kit. Most of the same supplies can serve either humans or dogs. The Kwik Stop sold in pet supply stores is actually an excellent styptic powder that can be used equally effectively on humans. Either Neosporin (sold for humans) or Panalog (sold for dogs) is a good antiseptic ointment for both species. Perhaps the only dog-specific item you may want to add to a first-aid kit is ear wash. If you want to buy a first-aid kit, check with your local Red Cross—some sell a nice kit enclosed in a travel-size pillow. Such double-duty items are much appreciated when space is limited.

You will need something with which to pick up after your dog when he has a bowel movement. Plastic bags are the most compact thing to carry. They can be sandwich-bag size (even if your dog is a moose, you can use as many as you need) or larger produce-bag size. There are not always garbage receptacles along trails; carrying a couple of zipper-lock bags lets you put filled bags in them and close them up to lock away odor and messiness until you reach an appropriate disposal site.

As a friend reminded me, old towels are essential to have on your trip. You will need to dry muddy paws or entire dogs before welcoming them into your tent. And really old, disposable towels are excellent for cleaning up the effects of too much excitement or an upset stomach. They can serve as pot holders for the cookstove, dew wipers and all sorts of things.

Bringing along a coat or sweater for your dog is a good idea. If you do all your camping in summer, you may think this unnecessary, but what Mark Twain once said—"The coldest winter I ever spent was a summer in San Francisco"—can be surprisingly true. Once the sun goes down, certain areas are known for quickly dropping temperatures and bone-chilling damp. Even long-coated dogs may feel cold if they are not used to being outdoors at night.

If your dog needs entertainment while traveling, or if you plan to leave him in camp or a kennel while you visit some local attraction, a favorite toy or some rawhide chews can help keep him content. A caution, however: If you tie your dog and give him a ball, the ball can easily roll beyond the reach of his rope and inflict ceaseless barking on the campground and much ill will on you upon your return.

You will have to be the judge of your dog's comfort level. If she will be happy sleeping on the ground, fine. But if she curls up under a blanket in a snuggle bed every night at home, you may want to bring that bed or at least the blanket. There are even sleeping bags for dogs. Be aware that dogs do indeed suffer from cold, and plan accordingly.

Finally, if your dog is crate-trained or used to being confined in an exercise pen, you may want to bring such equipment along. There will be times you do not want your dog underfoot (while cooking dinner on a ground-level grill, for example). Whatever method of confinement your dog is accustomed to will be easiest for her to accept. But if space in your vehicle is shoehorn-tight, a tie-out or even a long line will serve to keep your dog where you want her. The Flexi Company now makes a retractable tie-out similar in design to their Flexi-Leads. The tie-outs are helpful in keeping dogs from getting entangled in their lines. A trainer friend recommends using an old Flexi-Lead tied to a tree above ground level. This stirs up less dust as the dog moves around, but there will still be dirt, which can jam the Flexi mechanism, so don't use a new one. Be aware that many campgrounds require that at night dogs be inside the tent or vehicle with you.

How to Pack

I'm not going to presume to tell you how to load your vehicle with all your equipment from the ground up. But I do have a few tips regarding your dog.

First, allow a sufficient amount of space for your dog in the car or van. (The next chapter will discuss various measures of restraint while in the car, but even if you let your dog have her freedom, it won't mean much if there isn't enough room for her to lie down.) If your dog has spent her whole life riding on the front seat with her chin on your knee, suddenly relegating her to the back corner with no line of sight to you could cause problems.

Wherever your dog will ride, be sure that no part of your load will shift onto her during your travels. Bungee cords can be put to good use inside a car as well as out. Hearing objects tumbling across the car and your dog crying out in alarm while you are driving a narrow road (with no place to pull over) at high speed

Checklist for Supplies Your Dog Will Need on the Trail

____ Paperwork (health certificate, rabies certificate, dog license)

____ Spare collar and leash

____ Food and water bowls

____ Food—the dog's usual diet

____ Water from home

____ Medications (and list of medications)

____ Flea/tick powder/spray

____ Comb or brush, tweezers, scissors

____ Plastic bags

____ Old towels

____ Coat or sweater

____ First-aid kit

____ Toys and/or chews

____ Blanket/kennel mat/sleeping bag

____ Crate/exercise pen/tie-out

because a logging truck is hugging your bumper is not a pleasant experience.

Some pieces of equipment can be used to make a comfortable nest for the dog. For example, sleeping bags can be laid down flat or folded in half in the area the dog will occupy, rather than rolled up and stashed as part of the load. This decreases the amount you have to pack out of the dog's way, creates a definite space for the dog, and keeps your sleeping bag easily accessible.

Be sure other items you will need upon your arrival are equally accessible. You do not want to unpack an entire load to reach your tent. Of course, first-aid kits should always be directly at hand.

Keep packed food away from the dog. She may be a paragon of virtue at home, but traveling can be stressful and may result in unexpected behavior. You do not want to arrive at some remote camp to find that the dog has eaten your dinner. Rummaging through your dinner can also have ill effects on your dog.

Common sense and a little patience will be excellent guides in your packing.

On the Road

Not all dogs are natural-born travelers. Serling was about five months old when I adopted him, a gangly puppy with a mischievous smile. He was fine during the ride home, but a longer ride to visit the beach left him vomiting and decidedly unhappy. When he had recovered, he did enjoy the outing, but then there was the ride home. By stopping several times, we avoided further vomiting. I next had to face the question of how to include a carsick dog in our hiking and camping expeditions.

We started taking Serling along on errands and other short car trips, trying to build up his endurance. I can't say for sure whether the desensitization worked or whether he simply outgrew the problem, but his car sickness disappeared and he became an excellent traveling companion.

Car Sickness

If you are not in the habit of taking your dog with you in the car, don't wait until your trip and then load up for that first 300-mile segment. You could be in for a nasty surprise (several nasty surprises, actually).

Long before your planned departure, start taking your dog in the car with you. This is not only to assess your dog's tolerance for motion, but to provide another training opportunity. You will want your dog to understand where his place is and, if you are using some form of restraint, to become accustomed to it.

If your dog does suffer from motion sickness, you have several options. You can try the desensitization technique I mentioned above. Note how long it takes before your dog becomes ill. Make frequent trips within his limits, then try extending the time gradually. If this doesn't work and he doesn't grow out of it, you may need to confer with your veterinarian. The solution may be as simple as withholding food and water for several hours before you travel. Or you may need a prescription for tranquilizers or other medication.

In-Vehicle Restraint

There are as yet no laws requiring dogs to wear seat belts in cars (though seat belts for dogs do exist). Some states do, however, require that dogs riding in the beds of pickup trucks be either tied down or crated. Consider your options. If your dog is already crate-trained, then using the crate in the car will be easy. (If you plan to break up your camping with an occasional night in a motel, you will find that some establishments permit crate-trained dogs while excluding others.) Remember your plans for packing the car, and position the crate where it will be when you are actually traveling. Give the dog a view out a window and a sight line to you if at all possible. This will ensure that he gets a good flow of air, and he'll appreciate the scenery and the reassuring visual contact with you.

If you did not use a crate in training your dog, it is still a good traveling option. Many dogs accept being crated with little or no fuss. Choose a crate big enough for your dog to stand up, turn around, and lie down in. Line the bottom with a blanket that already belongs to your dog, or one of your old shirts. Put one or two of his favorite treats at the back of the crate. You may be surprised at how willingly your dog enters this new contraption, especially if you have

You can use your dog's leash to secure him to a spot on the back seat—make sure he's wearing a buckle and not a choke collar.

done a variety of things with your dog and taught him that if you are telling him to do it, it's safe. You will, of course, have to gradually work up the amount of time your dog spends in the crate, and your distance from it.

While crates work equally well in cars, vans or trucks (though they should be secured in place if in a truck), there are also other options for one or the other. Seat belts or car seats (for small dogs) can be used in cars and vans. Tie-downs can be used in pickups.

Seat belts for dogs consist of a harness that buckles into the car's seat belt system. The harness portion must be fitted to your dog.

This choice definitely requires some training. A dog that jumps around can quickly become tightly entangled in the seat belt. You need to help your dog to understand that he can sit up, lie down, and generally shift position to be comfortable, but mustn't try to dash from window to window or turn completely around. It is best to practice in your driveway and on some little-traveled roads so that you can stop and control your dog if he starts to get rambunctious.

Car seats for dogs are much the same as car seats for infants. Some are almost exactly the same, while others are more enclosed, like a crate. Most are height-adjustable, allowing the dog to see out the window, and all are for small dogs, some up to ten pounds, others up to twenty-five pounds.

Some people prefer not to restrain their dog, but use a car barrier to confine them to the rear of a station wagon or hatchback. This will keep them from interfering with the driver, but will not protect them from being thrown around during sudden stops or turns.

Truck tie-downs come in two main varieties. One connects a leash to an anchor generally placed toward the front and in the middle of the bed, allowing the dog to move in a semicircle. The other has a line or track across the bed near the front, anchored on both sides. A leash is attached so that it can slide back and forth along the line or in the track, letting the dog move back and forth. Whichever you choose, you do not want your dog to be able to look around the sides or over the top of the cab. Thrusting his head into the airstream can result in eye injuries, ear problems, or even cuts from flying pebbles. Also be aware that the metal back of a pickup truck can burn paws on a hot day. You may need a bed liner or attached blanket of some kind to keep the dog's feet off the metal.

Teach your dog to "wait" when you open the door so that he doesn't go
bounding out the second it's opened.

This dog owner likes lots of air and has cabled two pet guards together to provide a safe but wide-open window.

Dogs can entangle themselves in any type of leash, and tie-downs are no exception. You will need some practice with this form of restraint, keeping an eye on the dog and stopping to untangle and calm him down, if necessary.

You may, of course, choose to let your dog ride without any form of restraint (though this is a bad idea, even illegal in some states, for pickups). You will still want your dog to show some restraint of his own. Dogs jumping wildly around in a car have caused accidents. Even if you escape any tragic consequences, having a dog repeatedly crash into you or wave a hairy tail in your face can become rather maddening in the course of a long trip. Dogs can be taught to confine their activity to one portion of the car or even to lie down while riding in the car. You will want to be sure to teach your dog not to leap out of the car the second a door or hatch is opened. Always be sure that your dog will wait until you give the word, whatever it may be, before going through any open door.

How you want your dog to travel is (mostly) up to you. Give it some thought, and give yourself and your dog enough time to learn the rules.

Open Windows

Dogs rely on their noses to an extent we can hardly imagine. We may "smell those cows" while driving past a feed lot, but dogs may know about the deer that crossed the road last night, the woodchuck burrow in the embankment, and the river running a mile to the east. An open window is a delight of odors for the traveling dog. But there are limits.

We've all undoubtedly seen cars with windows open wide and a dog hanging eagerly out, maybe just his head, or maybe both front feet and half the body. His long ears are sailing in the wind, his eyes are narrowed, and he is practically grinning with delight.

While this imaginary dog may be having a grand time now, he may end up spending a night at the vet's. A sudden swerve or stop could catapult the dog from the car. Or he could become so excited at some passing scent that he vaults through the window on his own. Even if he remains in the car, the chance of injury still exists. Flying sand or pebbles or even bugs can lodge in those exposed eyes and ears. Even floating bacteria can find easy entry to the innocent dog's system.

It is best to open windows far enough only to allow airflow. Do not leave enough space for your dog's head. If you will be traveling in particularly warm areas, or if you just aren't happy with only a couple of inches of opening, you may want to invest in some pet guards for windows. These hard plastic devices slot over the top of a car window, fit accordion-style to the width, and fit into the door frame at the top. They allow you to open the window further without permitting the dog to lean out. Look for them in pet catalogs, supply stores or other discount stores.

If you are using a car barrier and your dogs are confined to the rear of the car, you can of course open the front windows as wide as you like.

Open windows also have consequences when the car is stopped. Dogs have been known to lunge through windows and snap at or even bite people walking by. People have also been known to reach into the car to "pet the nice dog." Windows open wide can result in a dog deciding to take himself for a walk and getting lost in a strange area.

Overheating

One major reason people leave windows open in a parked car is to keep the dog who's waiting in the car cool. This is risky in a variety of ways. First, it may not work. A car parked in the sun on a hot day, even with the windows open, can quickly become an oven. Dogs are not able to perspire to dispel heat to any great degree, only "sweating" through their tongues and pads. This puts them at a greatly increased risk for heatstroke. Plenty of dogs have overheated and died while their owners "only ran into the store for a minute."

Even air-conditioned RVs are not a safe refuge in which to leave a dog unattended. A professional handler once left many show dogs in an air-conditioned motor home while taking one dog into the ring for its class. The judging took some time. When the handler finally returned to the motor home, the generator had quit, the temperature inside the motor home had soared, and all the dogs were dead.

There simply is no safe way to leave a dog unattended in a vehicle when it's hot. In some states it is even against the law, and law enforcement officials may break a window in your car to free the dog.

Symptoms of heat stress include heavy panting, a rapid heartbeat, a dark red or purple tongue, and legs, ears and a nose that feel hot and dry. Signs of heatstroke include glazed eyes, weakness, vomiting, diarrhea, dehydration and pale gray lips. If you return to your

You'll want to hit plenty of rest stops on the way—for you and your dog(s).

vehicle to find your dog in distress, soak the dog's coat in cool water and massage the skin gently to encourage circulation. Check for dehydration by grasping a fold of skin from the middle of the dog's back and gently pulling it away from the dog. Let go. If the skin stays pulled away from the body when released, or slowly goes back to its original shape, the dog is dehydrated. Offer small amounts of cool water at spaced intervals.

If you camp with only your dog for company, you will need to plan ahead. Shopping will have to be done early or late, in the relatively cool periods of the day.

A parked car with open windows is also a target. Contrary to popular opinion, not all thieves are afraid of dogs, especially if the dog in question is leaning out of the car to lick the felon's face. Or your dog may be asleep in the back seat and not even visible. In either event, your dog may be stolen along with your car or dumped out along the way to fend for himself.

Even if theft is not the object, those open doors may prove too enticing to pass up. Someone could "let the dog out to play" or maliciously run the dog off. Objects such as rocks, bottles or fire-crackers could be thrown into the car.

Rest Stops

There are two extremes of drivers: One wants to stop at every vista point and roadside attraction; the other is bent on arriving at the designated destination in as little time as possible. Whatever your natural tendencies, try to stop and take your dog out for exercise at least every two hours. Not only will your dog appreciate it, the break will help keep you alert behind the wheel.

Be considerate in where you make your stops. Many highways have rest areas spaced out along them. Most of the rest areas have sections designated for dogs. Some are beautiful, with enticing trails leading off into woods. Others are weedy patches full of burrs, fleas and broken glass. You can only make the best of whatever conditions you find.

If there are no rest areas along your route, use scenic overlooks, pullovers, or anywhere it's safe to stop. Be sure and pick up after your dog.

Wherever you stop, don't just throw your dog back in the car the second he lifts his leg. Take a little stroll. Stretch those muscles, yours and his. Remember, you're on vacation!

Hazards of the Trail

Whether you only walk loops of a mile or less or hike far into the back country, a dog is an excellent trail companion. Remember to keep your dog's limitations in mind when setting out (and your own as well—unless you're on a loop or have someone driving to pick you up, you will have to walk out as far as you walk in). A pretrip health check and conditioning program (discussed in chapter 1) are prerequisites for safe and happy hiking. The following are conditions to consider or avoid once on the trail. I realize (and regret) that they can seem overwhelming. Please don't let them discourage you from taking your dog along, or from going camping entirely. Keep in mind that most people don't stop flying just because they have read news stories about airplane crashes. All the hazards discussed here are real and *could* happen, but they are unlikely to happen to you, especially if you know what to avoid.

Weather Hazards

Weather brings two obvious major problems: heat and cold.

The most serious consequence of hiking on **hot days** is the possibility of heat exhaustion. Your dog is a willing companion and will

Heat can severely affect your dog. In hot weather, stop often for rest and water. *Photo courtesy Tim and Wendy Paradis.*

probably do everything in her power to keep up with you. It's your reponsibility to see that there are no ill effects caused by her efforts. Be sure you both stop and drink often—from water you carry, not streams or puddles (discussed in the next section of this chapter).

Your dog is at a severe disadvantage in hot weather because she can sweat through only her tongue and paw pads. Watch for signs of heat distress: panting; rapid pulse; red gums; and legs, ears and nose that feel hot and dry. If your dog appears to be overheating, stop and rest in the shade. Wet your dog's head and the pads of her feet, if possible. Hike out slowly, stopping often.

More serious signs of heatstroke include glassy eyes, weakness, vomiting, diarrhea and dehydration. Check for dehydration by pulling up a fold of skin from the middle of the back. It should spring back into place when released. If it does not, the dog is dehydrated.

A dog showing these signs is in serious trouble. If you can, wrap the dog in a wet shirt or blanket and get her to a veterinarian promptly.

Consider the surface upon which you're hiking. Sand can get very hot. *Photo courtesy Kimberley Peterson.*

If the dog is too big to carry, do everything possible to cool her down. Wrap her in wet clothing and drip water into her mouth. *Do not* immerse her in a stream—the shock could kill her. Massage her skin gently to encourage circulation. Stay put in the shade, and give the water time to bring her temperature down. Walk out of wherever you are slowly, in the cool of evening, stopping often. Get to a vet as soon as you can.

Another consideration in hot weather is the surface on which you are hiking. Some trails are paved, and some pavement can get intensely hot. Consider your dog's feet. Reach down and rest your hand on the paved surface for several seconds. If it's uncomfortable for you, it probably will be for your dog. Choose a dirt trail instead, or save your walk for early morning, before the pavement has a chance to heat up.

One other possible effect of hot, sunny days comes as a surprise to most people. Light-skinned dogs can suffer from sunburn, especially

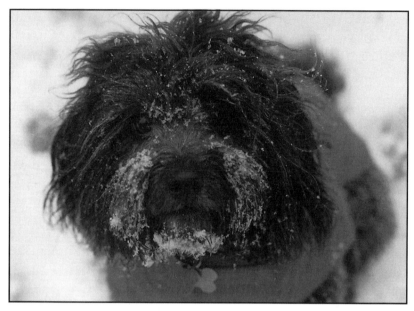

In cold, snowy conditions, your dog may appreciate wearing a sweater.

if they have had a long coat trimmed for the summer in a well-meaning effort to keep them cool. A dog's coat works as insulation in hot as well as cold weather and should not be clipped too close in any season. It is much more important to comb or brush a dog to remove loose undercoat.

You *can* use sunblock on dogs—especially on light-toned noses—but be sure it is nontoxic, as the dog is likely to lick it off. Otherwise, you will have to acclimate the dog gradually to sun exposure to avoid a burn. A terry-cloth coat can also help. This is a blanket cut from terry cloth, to extend over the dog's back and down her sides, with a strap across the chest and one under the belly. Soak the coat in cold water, and wring it out partially before you put it on the dog. It offers some protection from the sun and has a nice cooling effect on the skin.

Cold weather is a problem for some dogs. Short-coated, slightly built dogs such as Italian Greyhounds and Chihuahuas seem to suffer the most, but Dalmatians are also known to be easily chilled.

Dogs can shiver and their teeth can even chatter, but owners should offer help long before things get to this stage. There are all sorts of blankets, coats, and sweaters for dogs. Chosen well and fitted properly, they provide warmth and protection just as your coat does for you. It may take a little effort, however, to convince your dog that clothing is a good thing. Some dogs direct all their attention to getting rid of the offending garment; others simply become immobile, unwilling to take even one step. Get your dog used to any clothing (or any other new gear, for that matter) before leaving home.

Prolonged exposure to cold, especially if it is also wet, or an unexpected dunking in cold water, can result in hypothermia. Lethargy, indifference, uncontrollable shivering and even unconsciousness are symptoms. If your dog appears to be suffering from low body temperature, share your body heat with her in a sleeping bag or blankets. Have someone drive you to the nearest veterinarian while you attempt to warm the dog.

Even long-coated dogs that revel in playing, lying and even sleeping in the snow need some human assistance to keep warm. The dog's body temperature is regulated by the flow of air through the coat. This process is not efficient if the coat is dirty or matted. Keeping your dog combed or brushed is even more important in winter.

Frostbite also occurs in dogs, though it is rare. Ears, toes and scrotums are most susceptible, and older dogs with less efficient circulation are at increased risk. Symptoms are the same as in humans— red or pale skin, pain and itching. Warm the affected area gently, without rubbing, and get the dog to a vet to circumvent any permanent tissue damage.

Though four legs and a low center of gravity make dogs more secure than people on slippery surfaces, they can still slip and fall on ice. An awkward fall can result in sprains, pulled muscles or other injuries.

Cold weather also brings other problems. Ice can cut pads. Snow can freeze into ice balls between the pads. Paws that are constantly wet can develop fungal or bacterial infections. Road salt or chemicals used to de-ice roads can be extremely irritating (and if licked off can even cause internal damage and dehydration). If you are among the hardy band of winter campers, you probably already have boots for your dog. If you or your dog do not accept the idea of boots, then at least trim the fur around your dog's pads to help deter snow or ice buildup. Wash the pad regularly, and if the dog seems to be having problems, try rubbing petroleum jelly or baby oil on the pads. Also remember to wash ears or tummy fur if either drags in the snow.

One final winter hazard is often overlooked. A blanket of snow is pretty and fun to play in, but it alters scenery and deadens scent, and if your dog wanders off, she will have a harder time finding her way home. Pay close attention to your dog's whereabouts in a winter wonderland.

Dogs enjoy playing in the water, but be careful about the sources from which they drink. *Photo courtesy Tim and Wendy Paradis.*

Water is wonderful for dogs, but be aware of what lurks in and around it.

Water Hazards

Although many hikers, myself included, used to drink from mountain streams, this has become increasingly hazardous. What was once known as "backpacker's disease" or "beaver fever" has now reached even municipal water supplies. The culprit is a protozoa called *Giardia lamblia.*

That seemingly pure mountain stream is almost certainly infested with this microscopic organism. It can survive and prosper equally well in your dog's intestines or in yours.

In infected water, Giardia is encased in a cyst, a protective shell. Drinking the water or, in the case of dogs, even swimming in it and then licking their fur, results in the cyst being ingested. The acids in the dog's or human's stomach break open the cyst, and Giardia then assumes its active phase.

The protozoa attach themselves to the wall of the small intestine and begin a frantic series of cell divisions. Ten little cysts can become a million active trophozoites in less than two weeks.

Symptoms generally appear one to two weeks after exposure. The most common sign is diarrhea, and it can be sudden and severe; it may even be bloody. If not treated, the diarrhea can persist indefinitely. Though not generally fatal, it can cause weight loss and nutrient deficiencies.

Because some of the cysts pass through the system intact, giardiasis is highly infectious. Since it is also frequently misdiagnosed, it often has a chance to spread unchecked.

Antibiotics are prescribed to combat the protozoa. Flagyl (metronidazole) or Atabrine (quinacrine) are the usual choices. Each of these can cause vomiting and nausea in their own right, but they are considered 90 percent effective. Signs of reinfestation, however, may occur in stressful situations.

To avoid this widespread pest, you can carry your own water, boil water hard for at least five minutes, or use iodine tablets or filters specifically labeled as antigiardial. This is not a part of nature you want to experience firsthand.

Algae and Fungi

An even more bizarre-seeming hazard can lurk in water: **algae.** Though this is rare, I know of two reports of dogs who got sick and died after drinking water with a concentrated algae bloom. Algae produces an exotoxin called phytotoxin, which has disastrous effects when ingested in significant quantities. This is called algae intoxication.

The progression of events isn't completely understood, but the onset of symptoms is rapid. Vomiting, diarrhea and lethargy have shown up just an hour after the dogs drank the algae-laden water. There is no known antidote. If you're going to let your dog drink from lakes and streams, be sure they're at least *clear* lakes and streams.

Another little-heard-of disease is not actually in water but nearby. **Blastomycosis** is caused, again in both dogs and humans, by inhaling airborne spores of a fungus, *Blastomyces dermtitides*. Little is known about this potential hazard, but it seems to favor damp acid soils near streams and lakes. For reasons unknown, Wisconsin has the highest incidence of reported cases.

There is no vaccine to protect against it, but when blastomycosis is diagnosed and treated early, the rate of recovery is an impressive 95 percent. Untreated, this disease is nearly always fatal.

Symptoms can mimic pneumonia: a raspy bark, audible respiration, fever. Or there may be no obvious pulmonary symptoms (though the lungs are always infected), but the dog is lethargic and has no appetite. Oozing sores may develop anywhere on the body.

Diagnosis can be made by staining a sample from an oozing sore or by culturing a tracheal swab. Treatment includes administering IVs to counter dehydration and taking ketoconazol.

Histoplasmosis is the most common systemic fungal disease of dogs in the United States. It is found in the Mississippi River basin, the Great Lakes region and the St. Lawrence River valley. It seems to be associated with droppings from bats and starlings. Its symptoms are similar to those of other fungal infections, and definitive diagnosis may require a liver biopsy.

Aspergillus is found across the country, and both dogs and humans encounter its spores frequently, especially where there is decaying vegetation. But contact is usually benign. Occasionally dogs may develop lesions in the nose. A mucousy discharge may be a sign.

Coccidioidomycosis, also known as San Joaquin Valley fever, is found in soil in Texas, New Mexico, Arizona, California and Nevada, but only in the winter. During or after the rainy season, the fungus releases spores, which can then be inhaled. There are usually no effects, but older or ill dogs may exhibit a cough or labored breathing, persistent fever, loss of appetite and depression. Diagnosis is made with a tracheal wash.

All of these fungal diseases have been treated in the past with amphotericin B. With kidney damage as a very possible side effect, this drug had to be administered slowly, through an IV drip, over a period of six to eight weeks. This meant the dog had to be kept at the veterinary hospital for that period, a stressful experience for the dog and an expensive one for the owner.

The more recent drug of choice is ketoconozole. This treatment is administered initially by IV, but then switched to pill form, so the dog can recover at home.

With Giardia, algae intoxication, and all the fungal infections lurking in or near water, pay careful attention to *any* unusual canine behavior after visiting lakes, ponds, rivers or streams. If you suspect any problem, pay a visit to your veterinarian. After all, which is more important, trying to save a few dollars or saving your dog's life?

Drowning

There is of course one more hazard posed by water—drowning. People seem to have the idea that dogs don't drown, but that supposition is entirely incorrect. Not all dogs are the canine equivalent of Mark Spitz. Some simply don't swim very well. Even good swimmers can get into trouble in strong currents, undertows or very cold water. If you would not feel safe swimming in some location, don't assume it is safe for your dog.

The possibility also exists that the dog's collar will catch on an underwater branch or discarded fishing line or some other obstruction. A choke collar, with its dangling end, is particularly dangerous in this respect. Dogs should generally wear their ID collars all the time, but removing them before a swim may not be a bad idea (as long as you can control the dog without benefit of a collar and leash).

This looks like a pleasant enough walk, but the growth along both sides of the trail is foxtails, and the pointy seed heads are scattered everywhere.

Plant Hazards

Undoubtedly the most well-known hazard from plants is **foxtails.** But they are only one representative of the many pointed, barbed or sticky weed seeds you may encounter. Because many of these ingenious designs of nature are built to travel unrelentingly forward once they grab onto something, it is essential that you check your dog for burrs and other foreign objects after any venture into field or woods. Don't forget to check behind and inside ears and between pads.

I have always checked my dogs, but I must have gotten lazy about combing carefully through those long coats, because I once

Though your dogs won't get it, if they come in contact with poison ivy, you can get it by touching them.

missed a foxtail on Spirit. Several weeks later the vet dug it out, and poor Spirit had a shaved flank and two drains to clear up the abcess it had made. Fortunately it didn't penetrate any internal organs. I've never been lazy about that particular chore again.

In the Southwest, especially for dogs visiting from other areas, **cactus** can be a problem. **Jumping cholla** seems to leap at passing pooches (and people). **Thorns** may litter the ground, waiting for unwary paws. Even worse, birds nest in the cactus, an enticement for dogs to investigate. If your dog is not cactus-wise, be especially cautious in the desert.

Farther north, you may encounter **stinging nettles** and **Canadian thistles.** These contain a toxin that causes an itchy rash. Be sure to comb them out of your dog's coat and see that none are lodged in his feet.

Another serious danger is plants that are poisonous if eaten. There are too many to detail here, from baneberry to wild cherry, bracken to yew. Different plants grow in different parts of the country. It is not a bad idea to know those most common in your area. One of the most widespread (and generally viewed as innocuous) is the **acorn.** This squirrel favorite is toxic to dogs if eaten. Symptoms include vomiting, darkened diarrhea and black gums. Death can result. The various toxins in poisonous plants may attack the heart, liver, kidneys, nervous system, or digestive tract. The best prevention is to be sure that your dog doesn't do any grazing along the trail.

Finally, there's one plant hazard that affects humans rather than dogs. It appears that dogs are largely immune to **poison oak, poison sumac** and **poison ivy.** But they can pick up the irritating sap on their coat and transfer it to their unsuspecting owners. If you are prone to breaking out in those itchy irritating bumps, make every effort to keep your dog out of the brush. Otherwise, petting your dog could result in hours of itching and scratching for you.

Insects

You obviously don't have to go on a camping expedition for your dog to pick up **fleas.** At one time or another, they are a problem for most pet owners not living on a mountaintop (fleas do not prosper at altitudes above 5,000 feet). But the fleas encountered in the wild can carry diseases not usually found in more civilized areas.

In the Sierra Nevada and other isolated sections of the country, **bubonic plague** is endemic in the rodent population. It can be transmitted by the fleas that the rodents carry. Signs warn campers to stay well away from ground squirrel burrows, a difficult proposition since the holes often riddle the campgrounds. Campers and hikers should certainly not allow their dogs to stick their noses down burrows.

Applying a safe flea repellent to your dog before venturing into the wild can help ensure that he does not pick up any unwanted parasites. Consult your veterinarian about which product to use and how often it can be applied.

Ticks have been much in the news over the last several years. As **Lyme disease** has spread across the country, research has shown that

Fleas and ticks lurk in long grass, woods and most areas. Apply a safe insect repellent to yourself and your dog before you venture out. *Photo courtesy Tim and Wendy Paradis.*

it is not just the deer tick that is the culprit. There are now half a dozen types of ticks implicated as vectors of this disease. The actual culprit is the bacterium *Borrelia burgdorferi.* Symptoms in dogs, much as in humans, may include fever, sudden and severe lameness, swelling in the joints, and lethargy. A vaccine to prevent Lyme disease in dogs has been developed but has not yet gained widespread acceptance, though it is proving effective where used.

Ticks also carry other equally nasty diseases, such as Rocky Mountain spotted fever. This disease is caused by the agent *Rickettsia rickettsii* and is transmitted by the Rocky Mountain wood tick. The diseases cause fevers of 104 degrees or more, loss of appetite, and listlessness. Treatment with the antibiotic tetracycline usually provides quick relief.

Mosquitoes carry heartworm, and are especially bad at dawn and dusk in July and August. *Photo courtesy Tim and Wendy Paradis.*

Another tick-borne disease is **tularemia.** A bacterium, *Francisella tularensis*, causes this affliction, which causes fever, swollen lymph nodes, and bleeding from the nose. Tetracycline is usually given to treat tularemia.

Ehrlichiosis is another dangerous tick-transmitted disease that depletes all the cells in the victim's body, especially red blood platelets. It's carried by the brown dog tick, which is most commonly found in southwestern states. Symptoms are loss of appetite and weight loss, lethargy, swollen lymph nodes along the back or legs, occasional stumbling or limping, and nosebleeds. It's important for owners to recognize the symptoms early, as ehrlichiosis that progresses to the nosebleed stage is often fatal. Owners are best advised to keep ticks off their dogs and to have a blood test taken for ehrlichiosis when returning from a tick-infested area. People cannot get the disease from dogs, or vice versa.

Even without the presence of disease, an infestation of ticks can result in a reaction called tick paralysis. A neurotoxin that comes from the tick's salivary gland works slowly on the dog's system. Ticks attached along the spinal column or neck seem more likely to create problems, and a single tick can have dire consequences. A week to nine days after the tick attaches and begins to feed, symptoms appear. The dog may be lame and listless and may not be able to bend down to drink. He may also have a high temperature. Removal of the tick(s) brings marked improvement within twenty-four hours. Reinfestation can result in another attack, so owners are advised to bathe and dip dogs prone to tick infestation every few weeks. (Consult with a veterinarian.) Failure to remove the parasite(s) from an infected dog will result in death from respiratory paralysis.

Good insect repellents can deter ticks from attaching to your dog—and to you. If you return to your home after a hike, a bath with a good flea and tick shampoo can get rid of most external parasites that may have ridden home on your dog. If you find a tick that has already embedded its head in your dog, do not touch it. Use tweezers to grasp the tick as close to the mouth parts as possible, and pull back with a steady firm pressure. Drop the detached tick in alcohol, and take it to your vet for possible identification.

Yet another pest to be aware of is the **mosquito.** While a mosquito bite may be merely annoying to you, the consequences for your dog can be much more severe. Mosquitoes can carry the dreaded **heartworm,** which is known scientifically as *Dirofilaria immitis.* The months of highest prevalence are July and August, prime camping time. Fortunately, infestation is easily avoided by keeping your dog on one of the monthly or daily oral preventatives available from your veterinarian.

Bees and wasps are also threats. Perhaps the greatest risk to your dog is stumbling into a yellow jacket nest. One type of these wasps lives in holes in the ground, so they are more at the dog's level. They are also quicker to sting than almost any other bee or wasp, and can sting repeatedly, unlike bees. In some of the southern areas of the country, killer bees have arrived. These short-tempered bees are known for attacking in swarms, and several dogs in Arizona have been stung to death. Even a single sting to the head, nose or throat can cause enough swelling to make breathing difficult.

If you or your dog has been stung, scrape out the stinger—grabbing and pulling will force added venom into the wound. Pack the area in ice, cold water, or mud. If your dog has received multiple stings, take her to a veterinarian in case of allergic reaction.

Also be aware that bees or wasps can become entangled in a dog's coat. You may be the one who gets stung trying to help.

In the Southeast, the landscape is dotted with **fire ant** nests, some as high as two feet tall! But many nests are not so obvious. Stumbling into one, whether it's you or your dog, can result in a swarm of angry biting ants. Treat the bites the same as you would a bee sting.

Snakes, Scorpions, Spiders and Lizards

There are four poisonous snakes in the United States: the **copperhead, coral snake, cottonmouth** (also known as the water moccasin) and **rattlesnake.**

The coral snake is least likely to be encountered. It is the only U.S. poisonous snake that is not a pit viper. Its venom is a neurotoxin, related to cobra venom. Fortunately, it is small, shy, found only in the extreme southeast, and unlikely to be a problem. It looks decidedly like the harmless king snake, so unless you are very sure of your identification, stay away from all brightly striped snakes.

The other three are all pit vipers, denoted by the small holes (pits) partway up their faces. Their venoms are similar, causing symptoms such as swelling at the bite location, vomiting, dizziness, nosebleeds, convulsions and coma. If your dog is bitten, identify the snake if you can, but don't waste time over it. Keep the dog warm and quiet, and get to a veterinary hospital as quickly as possible.

The cottonmouth is fearless and will rarely bother to retreat. It lives in swamps, bayous, ditches, rice fields and near lakes and ponds. It is an excellent swimmer.

The copperhead favors fields and can easily be trod on by unsuspecting dogs and humans. They are slow to move out of the way.

Rattlesnakes of one kind or another are found nearly everywhere in the United States, from deserts to mountaintops. (Surprisingly, there are no rattlers—indeed, no poisonous snakes of any kind—on Washington's Olympic Peninsula.) Contrary to popular belief, they do not always rattle before striking. They can bite without injecting poison, or deliver a full load—there is no way of knowing until symptoms appear.

Many dogs seem to have an inborn fear of snakes and will do everything possible to avoid them. I once stepped on a long stick, moving the other end, which happened to be near my Keeshond. Sundance vaulted straight into the air, then somehow managed to move sideways three feet or more before coming back to earth. When she discovered that it was a stick, not a snake, she gave me a dirty look—insults to her dignity were nearly always deemed to be my fault.

In some areas of the country, you may encounter scorpions and poisonous spiders. Some scorpions are poisonous; some are not. The poisonous variety is found in Arizona, New Mexico, and California along the Colorado River. With the poisonous sting, there is immediate pain. The dog may seem restless and agitated, with jerky head or eye movements.

The two **poisonous spiders** found in the United States are the brown recluse and the black widow. The bite of the brown recluse is notorious for killing skin in the area of the bite. The region swells and turns black, fills with blood and ruptures, leaving an ulcer. A skin graft may be required, and the entire healing process can take months. A black widow bite is more deadly. The dog may seem overexcited and shiver intensely. There may be seizures, breathing trouble, and uncontrolled salivation.

These pests usually prefer to avoid confrontations, but if your dog is the type who sticks her nose under every bush and stone, keep her close by your side, away from temptation. Depending on your dog's size and susceptibility to the poison, a bite or sting could be fatal.

Many people have heard of the nation's only **poisonous lizard,** the Gila monster. But it is exceedingly unlikely that you will encounter one, even if you are camping in the desert.

If your travels take you to southern Texas or southern Florida, you may well come across **Bufo toads.** These fat, lethargic creatures do not have nearly the reputation of the Gila monster, but they are much more likely to cause problems. They secrete a thick, milky poison over their back. The unfortunate dog who bites or even licks one can be dead in fifteen minutes. Symptoms include seizures, irregular heartbeat, and coma. If you suspect your dog has tasted a Bufo toad, rinse her mouth with water and induce vomiting. Seek medical help but be prepared to administer CPR yourself.

Inducing Vomiting in Dogs

Every first-aid kit should include syrup of ipecac. Use one teaspoon for every ten pounds of canine body weight. To give it to your dog, pull back her bottom lip near the corner of the mouth and trickle the syrup into the pocket while holding the dog's head up. Syrup of ipecac takes somewhat longer to act on dogs than it does on humans, but it does work. The dose may need to be repeated if results are not achieved with the first try.

Small Animals

One of the dire possible consequences of contact with wild animals is rabies. Keep well away from any animal exhibiting unusual behavior,

Deer are a common sight on many hikes or camping trips.

such as fearlessness, or from noctural creatures out and about in daylight. Even if your dog has been vaccinated against rabies, it is not 100 percent effective; rabies infection is still a possibility. At present, the areas most afflicted with rabies are the East Coast, south Texas, and southern California. Other problems—plague carried by fleas, ticks of all sorts—have been discussed previously. But there's more.

Rats and mice and their high-country cousin, the pica, carry a whole host of diseases besides rabies: distemper, leptospirosis, anthrax, tularemia, murine typhus, salmonella, rickettsial pox, Rocky Mountain spotted fever and rat-bite fever. Some are transmitted by external parasites, as already discussed. Others are passed through a bite (either rodent biting dog, or dog biting rodent, even if the rodent is already dead). Some may be contracted simply by sniffing infected urine. It cannot be overemphasized that the safest course is to keep your dog well away from all forms of wildlife.

Rabbits, though they generally offer no direct harm to a dog themselves, can certainly lead a dog astray quite literally. A dog chasing a rabbit can get lost in a hurry.

Years ago, Spirit and Serling were accompanying me in the Nevada desert. We were visiting some archaeological sites in the cool of morning. Since we were really in the middle of nowhere and the dogs had been responding well to commands, I let them off-leash. No sooner did I do so than a jackrabbit sprang up under their noses and they were off! Now totally oblivious to commands, they disappeared around the foot of a large hill and were gone.

Of course I hurried after them. But by the time I rounded the hill they were nowhere to be seen, despite the general openness of the terrain. I was truly frightened that I would never see either dog again. But I was lucky. They returned on their own, tired but happy, their tongues lolling out, not a bit contrite for their disobedience. No damage done—other than to my nerves. (I did fortunately smarten up about off-leash dogs before anything bad ever happened,

Chipmunks and ground squirrels, like their cousins mice and rats, can carry a slew of pests and diseases.

but it seemed to take a lot of near mishaps before it penetrated my head that even seemingly well-trained dogs do not always respond to commands when something more interesting happens.) More training has given me more control and some useful hints. Trainer friend Mandy Book offers the useful, potentially life-saving suggestion that "NO" shouted really loudly will often stop a dog dead in his tracks when other commands don't work.

If a dog catches a rabbit or hare (and some do get lucky now and then), or finds a carcass and nibbles on that, the unhappy result can be liver flukes or tularemia. And of course the external parasites will desert the dead bunny and make a new home on your dog, perhaps bringing tapeworm along with them.

Skunks, knowing well the effectiveness of their line of defense, will often amble about in plain sight. Dogs not aware of what lies in store can be in trouble. Given the opportunity, skunks will usually issue a warning before they spray. When a skunk stamps its front feet, make tracks, because its next action will probably be to raise its tail and let the victim have it.

If your dog takes a blast directly in the face, remember that skunk spray is akin to mace. Wash your dog's eyes out if she will let you. For the awful aroma, a commercial product called Odormute (available through pet supply stores) and that old folk remedy tomato juice are the most effective solutions. If a campground store is your only source of supply, tomato juice may be all that's available. Wet your dog first with dish soap and rinse, then soak her with the juice and leave it on for fifteen or twenty minutes before rinsing. If the odor is still bad, do it again.

Opossums, though they have a stunning mouthful of teeth, are pacifists. They will generally try to escape or try to play dead. But they will fight if attacked, and those teeth are excellent weapons. They also seem to carry more fleas, ticks and mites than most other animals, and even near encounters can transfer some of these to your dog.

Raccoons seem to be born with a loathing for dogs, and are willing and vicious fighters. Large boar coons can outweigh many spaniels. There are tales of raccoons luring dogs to water and then holding them under and drowning them. Even without the added hazard of water, raccoons can use all four feet to hold onto an opponent, leaving their jaws free to find a better, deadlier grip. More than a few dogs have been killed in encounters with raccoons. Even if a dog survives a fight, he may have been infected with parvovirus, distemper or leptospirosis. Rabies is reaching epidemic proportions in the raccoon population in the northeastern United States. They may be cute, with their masks and humanlike hands, but raccoons are no friends to dogs.

Porcupines are fat and slow and easy to avoid. But uneducated dogs usually do not realize that they are to be avoided. While it is a myth that porcupines can throw their quills, they do lash out with their quill-laden tail. The quills are barbed and once lodged must be pushed through and the barb cut off, or cut out. Quills left in the

Keeping your dog(s) on-leash and close to you can help you both avoid potential hazards.

victim continue to work forward and can eventually pierce a vital organ and cause death. Unless you are an old hand at it, quill removal is best left to a veterinarian.

Be aware that, odd as it may seem, dogs do not necessarily learn anything from such painful encounters. While some dogs will ever after go to great lengths to avoid porcupines, others will rush in time after time, never seeming to understand cause and effect.

Though not usually thought of as a threat, eagles, hawks, vultures and owls can all prey on small dogs. I have read reports of a Dachshund attacked on a beach by a bald eagle and a Poodle in grasslands swooped down on by a hawk. If your dog is rabbit-sized, be aware that danger can lurk in the skies.

Elk are imposing at all times and, during the autumn rut, can be ill-tempered.

Large Animals

Mention danger from a large animal and for some reason most people think of **bears.** It's true that dogs don't seem to like bears and the sentiment is returned. And it's possible that a dog running ahead of you could surprise a bear and, if the dog has any sense, turn tail and run, leading that now-angry bear straight back to you. But there are a lot of other animals you are more likely to encounter. If you know you are in bear country, wear bear bells, make noise, and keep your dog with you on-leash.

In the Southeast, from the Carolinas to Florida to Texas, a very real hazard is posed by **alligators.** These ungainly looking creatures are actually very fast for short distances and can surprise unwary dogs. Stay well away from waterways that could be home to alligators.

Another animal you are not very likely to encounter is the **badger.** A badger backed into a corner is a savvy fighter, using his great sickle claws and sharp teeth. A dog taking one on is likely to be mauled or killed.

People think of **deer** as pretty, shy, timid woodland creatures. Generally they are. But during rutting season, they can become aggressive, and they know how to use those sharp hooves and horns. Their larger relations, **elk and moose,** are less timid, sometimes bad-tempered, and even more capable of doing serious damage to a dog. With deer there is the additional hazard that in many parts of the country a dog caught running deer can be shot on sight.

There are a couple of kinds of wild cats in the country, but it is rare to even catch a glimpse of them. The compact **bobcat** and larger **cougar** are both extremely shy and will try their best to avoid being seen. But like all cats, they have an arsenal of sharp claws and teeth and will fight hard if cornered.

Our dogs also have two wild cousins. The **coyote** can be found nearly everywhere. The **wolf** is much more rare, but has been making its way back into some of the more isolated areas of the country. Coyotes are seen fairly often, but are not generally a problem. They may, however, be attracted to a bitch in heat or to food left around your campsite. These wild canids are relatives of our dogs, and are susceptible to all the same diseases and able to pass them to your pet.

In some places, letting your dog approach wildlife can have additional, monetary consequences for you. There are local and federal laws protecting all sorts of wild animals, and even approaching too closely can be considered harassment. The fines are hefty. Always keep your dog well away from all wildlife.

Finally, something not usually considered a hazard is livestock. It is common practice to graze cattle and sheep on public lands. Any dog caught worrying livestock can legally be shot.

Other People

Human activity poses a variety of possible wilderness problems for you and your dog.

First, know hunting seasons where you will be traveling. Though many hunters are responsible, conscientious people, some will shoot at any sound or movement. If hiking in an area open to hunting, keep your dog close at your side, wear non-natural bright colors, and talk or sing loudly to identify yourself as a human. There are also bright orange vests made for dogs to wear to help make them visible and obviously not a game animal. It is much wiser to simply avoid open-hunting areas.

Humans create more hidden nonseasonal problems, though. Discarded materials are often dumped on public lands, and some can be quite dangerous. Broken glass is an obvious problem. But discarded barbed wire is even more serious. It can entangle an animal and inflict severe cuts as the animal struggles to free itself. There are also pop-top tabs and, around water, fishhooks and fishing line. It is a sad comment on our civilization that you can hardly go anywhere without encountering trash of one kind or another.

Discarded foods may be extremely attractive to dogs, but can cause problems if eaten. Even droppings left by other dogs, or by wild dogs, though of great interest to your dog, can contain and pass along parasites.

Poison bait may be put out by ranchers (though this is currently illegal) or by disturbed individuals. Leg-hold traps may be set out and well-camouflaged, and can catch humans as well as dogs.

Check to see what activities are allowed on any trails you plan to hike. Some are open to motorized vehicles and can be as dangerous as walking down a roadway. Even mountain bikes can result in a fatal collision. Choose carefully and know what you may encounter.

Though this is a long and perhaps daunting list of potential mishaps, a great number of them can be avoided simply be keeping your dog on-leash at your side. This also keeps your dog from wandering too close to the crumbly edges of bluffs or bounding up rocky slopes you have no intention of climbing, from chasing off after other dogs, from spooking horses encountered on the trail, and all sorts of mischief. It also allows you to watch your dog's response to her surroundings, a pleasure discussed in the next chapter.

By all means, enjoy hiking with your canine companion—it takes only a little common sense to ensure that the experience is a happy one.

Pleasures of the Trail: Sharing the Experience

s I have mentioned, a dog is an excellent trail companion, enjoying your company, savoring the great outdoors. But if we pay attention to their responses to their surroundings, our dogs can also help us notice wildlife we might not otherwise see. And of course just watching them enjoy themselves so fully is a joy in itself. A friend relates that her clearest memory of her first camping trip is of her small dog posed on top of a rock, the wind blowing back her long ears. My favorite photo of my Keeshond, Sundance, is also in the woods on a rock, furry head and tail nearly meeting over her back, fox ears swiveled in two different directions. Dogs seem to gain an extra ounce of vibrancy when out in the wild, and it is a pleasure to see.

Understanding how your dog's basic senses differ from your own can help you experience a little of what your dog is taking in. But only a little. Imagination will have to supply the rest.

How Dogs See

The actual fine details of how a dog sees vary according to facial makeup. Sighthound-type dogs such as Afghans and Salukis have

You can "see" and experience many other pleasures of the outdoors through your dog's senses.

their eyes set forward. Guarding-type dogs such as German Shepherd Dogs and Great Pyrenees have their eyes set more to the side. The placement has a great impact on how the dog actually sees.

Sighthounds, meant to keep prey in sight and give chase, have relatively good binocular vision based on the position of their eyes and their long narrow muzzles, which do not block their sightline. But they are still farsighted, as are all dogs. No type of dog can see something right in front of his nose really well.

Guard dogs need to see a wide sweep of territory, so their eyes are set more to the side, decreasing binocular vision but greatly increasing their peripheral field. The average human with good peripheral vision can see an arc of 180 degrees. The canine field of vision can be as much as 250 degrees.

Because of their size, shape and physical makeup, a dog's eyes see things ours don't. *Photo courtesy Tim and Wendy Paradis.*

Some terriers and Nordic breeds have their eyes set in a relatively forward position, but slanted. This arrangement makes the best of binocular and peripheral vision, letting them see around the corners of their own heads.

But it is more than just eye position that sets canine sight apart from human sight. A dog's eye is more flattened, helping to make it more sensitive to light and movement but less able to resolve. There is an additional layer, the tapetum lucidum, beneath the rods and cones of the retina. This opaque layer reflects light back to the rods and cones, increasing the ability to see in decreased light. It is also the reason that dogs' eyes shine at night.

Dogs have a high number of rods, responsible for seeing in low levels of light (cats have even more). It was once thought that they had no cones, the basis for seeing in color. This view has shifted. It is now known that dogs do have cones and can see basic color, but this is not considered to be important to them.

The dog's eye is built to register movement above all else. A dog is ten times more sensitive than a human to peripheral movement. A Sheepdog can register and respond to her master's arm movement from a mile away. The tradeoff is that they can't see something directly in front of their nose.

Out on the trail, this sensitivity to movement and the wide field of vision allows your dog to see wildlife that you would miss. For wild canines, this is of course essential for survival. For you and your domesticated canine, it simply means the opportunity to see more wild creatures.

Watch your dog. If he indicates sudden interest, look where his nose and ears point. He probably caught movement that he is now trying to verify with other senses. It may not be spectacular—a mouse or squirrel is every bit as interesting to a dog as a deer or an elk—but it probably will be something alive and moving.

How Dogs Hear

A dog can hear about eight and a half octaves, roughly the same as humans. But their hearing range is shifted to a higher scale. The average person's hearing stops at around 20,000 cycles per second. Dogs can hear up to 40,000 cycles per second. This serves a very useful purpose in the wild—mice and voles squeak in this higher range. Wild canines can hear those squeaks, and small rodents form the staple diet of at least some wild canines.

Dogs of course also have the advantage of having mobile ears. Prick-eared dogs have the biggest advantage, but all dogs can swivel their ears to better locate and collect interesting sounds. It is estimated that dogs can hear sounds at roughly four times the distance humans can.

To coordinate the information coming in from two separate sources, a dog has a great portion of his brain devoted to analyzing sound. Experiments have shown that dogs can differentiate between

Note the alert ear position on this dog, and her intent gaze in the same direction.

sounds varying by only one-eighth of a tone, which probably explains how your dog can identify you coming home in your car before you are even in sight. It may also verify that dogs can and do enjoy music.

When you are out in a natural environment, watch how your dog's ears swivel in different directions, searching for sounds of interest to them. Then watch those ears focus in on something. This is often accompanied by the most gorgeous pose of total alertness. You can try and spot whatever it is your dog is hearing, or simply enjoy the picture of your dog enjoying herself.

How Dogs Smell

More has been written about the dog's sense of smell than any of the other senses, undoubtedly because we use the dog's nose for sports

The dog's nose is an amazing organ, infinitely more sensitive than ours.

such as tracking and scent hurdles, and serious pursuits such as drug sniffing and search and rescue. But even with all the attention, a dog's sense of smell remains shrouded in mystery simply because it is so far superior to our own feeble abilities.

Here are some examples of how great this ability is:

Do your dogs get excited when you're still a mile or more away from your destination on a trip to the beach? A dog can smell a teaspoon of salt in thirteen gallons of water.

Dogs love to be petted, which fulfills their need for touch.

Wonder how a dog can find a buried bone? Unless he's dug more than two feet deep, he can smell it right through the earth.

In an experiment in the 1920s, a person held a stick for two seconds. The stick was then handled by four other people and placed among a group of twenty other sticks, some unhandled, some touched by one or more of the four people. A dog allowed to scent the person who initially handled the stick never failed to select the only stick that person had touched.

A later experiment, from the 1960s, found that a dog given the scent of progesterone, a female hormone, could select objects handled by a woman in the postovulation stage of her menstrual cycle (when the hormone is at its highest concentration). This would seem to confirm the long-held claim of dairymen that their dogs could reliably point out a cow in estrus.

This ability to smell is of course based on physical characteristics. Where we humans have 5 million scent receptors in our poorly equipped noses, a dog has 220 million. On this numerical basis alone, a dog's sense of smell might be thought to be forty-four times as acute as a human's. But such is not the case. The dog's capabilities range from 100 thousand to 100 million times better than a human's.

There are further reasons. Humans have roughly between one and two square feet of nasal membranes. Dogs have nearly nine square yards worth, an area larger than their entire body surface. Dogs also have nasal structures that are completely absent in humans—for example, the vomeronasal organ, which is not well-understood but is connected to scent.

A bony structure named the subeth moidal shelf is better understood. When a dog "sniffs," an air intake completely different from his normal breathing pattern, the air passes over this subeth moidal shelf and is not washed out when the dog exhales. So the odor molecules remain in the nose, resting on odor receptor cells. From there, the odor is converted to an electrical signal and sent to the brain.

As much as one-eighth of the dog's brain is devoted to smell, and there are direct connections from the nose to the parts of the brain regulating eating, drinking and sexual activity.

The author's dog, Serling, knows exactly when dinnertime is, and is not shy about letting her know it's time to be fed.

With all this finely tuned equipment, dogs can detect and identify odors too dilute to be measured by scientific instruments. Given their choice, they prefer odors of animal origin. Imagine what enjoyment hiking a trail through the woods or desert, with the scent trails of all the animal residents, must be!

Anyone familiar with dog breeds knows that scenting ability can differ widely. The Bloodhound is typically acknowledged as having the best canine nose, but he is a specialist, focusing on ground trailing. Other breeds, most notably the Collie, are better at air scenting. If you've ever tried to compete in Obedience with a Beagle, you understand why the breed is often described as "a foot tall and all nose." In fact, in an experiment from the 1960s, Beagles let loose in a one-acre field located the single mouse occupant in one minute. A pack of Fox Terriers took fifteen minutes. A group of Scotties never did find the mouse (probably more from lack of interest than from deficient scenting ability).

One final example may give you some indication of how effective a dog can be in this pursuit. Butyric acid is a component of human sweat. One gram of butyric acid (a tiny amount, to be sure) dissolved in the air over a city the size of, say, Pittsburgh, would be detected by a dog flying over in an open-cockpit biplane at an altitude of 300 feet. What an interesting (and smelly) world it must be to our dogs!

If you find all of this interesting and would like to see your dog's nose in action beyond hiking with him, you may want to look into search-and-rescue work. There are groups nearly everywhere across the country. Much of their work involves finding people lost in the outdoors, and you enjoy being out there or you wouldn't be reading this book!

Other Canine Senses

The first sense to actually develop in the puppy is touch. Still blind and deaf, puppies will seek out contact with warm, soft objects. A puppy deprived of touch will nearly always develop into a neurotic adult. This whole-body sense of touch is part of what makes petting so pleasant to the dog. But our canine friends also have something we humans do not—vibrissae. These stiff sensory whiskers located around the muzzle and above the eyes sense air flow.

Taste is one of the areas where we have distinctly more refined equipment than our dogs. Where we have some 9,000 taste buds, dogs have only 1,700. With dogs, odor and texture are actually far more important than taste where food is concerned. It is thought that dogs probably react to food as pleasant, neutral or unpleasant (rather than our sweet, salty, sour, bitter).

Body rhythms are a sense not often discussed. But the dog's "internal clock" is a very interesting mechanism. Anyone responsible for feeding a dog knows that as dinnertime approaches, the dog will be beside you focusing pleading eyes upon you, or he may actually present his food bowl to be filled. No one knows whether the dog naturally has a biological clock similar to our own or whether he adjusts his internal timing to our life-style, but the result is the same. In experiments, dogs have been accurate within one minute in a twenty-four-hour cycle. But they can also track longer time spans. In quarantine kennels where visits are on a regular weekly or monthly basis, kennel workers have noted that dogs alter their activities on the appointed day, anticipating the visit. What this means on the practical level is that no matter how hectic things may be when setting up camp, the dog will expect his dinner to be on time.

Even further out on the theoretical plane is ESP (Extra Sensory Perception). It is not yet fully accepted as existing in humans. Does it exist in dogs? It's very hard to sort out what may be based on acknowledged senses that are far more refined than our own and what might be some sort of "sixth sense." There are well-documented cases of dogs finding their way home across hundreds of miles of unknown territory. Are they using the angle of the sun's rays (the currently favored theory for how birds migrate) or the earth's electromagnetic fields (as it is

Keeping Your Dog Stimulated

Sensory stimulation is absolutely necessary for dogs, especially when they are young. Sensory input actually causes nerve cells to grow and make new synaptic connections in the brain. Dogs left on their own too long and too often will try to create their own sensory stimulation, which nearly always results in what we call destructive behavior. Even a well-behaved dog, if left locked in a car or RV all day while you are off touring, may make his own entertainment to the detriment of your vehicle. Understanding your dog's needs and training can help you and your dog through those times when he has to amuse himself—nondestructively.

postulated that whales do in their migrations)? Or is it something else? No one knows.

Studies are ongoing of dogs and other animals warning of impending earthquakes. There just may be electrostatic changes in the atmosphere before an earthquake, and animals may be able to detect them. But then again, maybe not.

One of the most interesting new developments is to use a dog's senses to assist humans with epilepsy. It was realized accidentally that certain dogs became agitated before a human of their acquaintance had an epileptic seizure. A few dogs have now been trained to warn their owners of an approaching episode, giving the person time to reach a safe position to ride out the seizure. People suffering from epilepsy have stated that this "early warning system" has allowed them much greater freedom and made a major improvement in their lives. Interestingly, this sensing ability seems to be hereditary.

As my dog Serling grows older, I am conducting my own highly unscientific experiment in the world of dog senses. Serling has always come to comfort me whenever I have been upset, even from another room. He still does it even though he is now going slowly deaf. So I can eliminate any sounds I may be making as a cue. Does he smell the salt water in tears? Possible, I guess. I'll never know for sure, but senses so far different from our own are endlessly fascinating.

Canine Communication

Dogs, both wild and domestic, communicate visually and vocally. We would do well to learn the basics of their language while we try to teach them ours.

Dogs use the position of their tails, ears and entire body to reveal their emotional state. Everyone should recognize the play bow, where the front half of the body is lowered to the ground while the rear end waggles in the air. But other postures are more often misunderstood.

A wagging tail indicates many different emotions, depending on its carriage, speed of movement, and other body indicators. A tail that is wagging in a lowered position, near or between the back legs, indicates nervousness or fear, especially if the head is also lowered. A tail raised high with just the tip waving slowly indicates a challenge posture, a possible threat. Reading your dog's body language could give you additional clues to what unseen animals your dog may be scenting.

Dogs also have quite a wide verbal repertoire. Wolf researcher David Mech has observed that, contrary to popular belief, wolves do bark, nearly always when strangers approach the pack. They also whine in greeting other pack members or when curious about something, and they growl in disputes over food. But their most versatile vocalization is the howl, as unique to each wolf as a fingerprint. Wolves in the wild often take part in a group howl before going out on a hunt, in an equivalent of the "break" coming out of a football huddle. When separated, they howl to reunite the pack. Individual howls are also passed along from wolf to wolf, communicating something in a telegraph system. And a wolf on his own will howl out his loneliness.

While dogs still howl (some more than others), the bark has become the mainstay of their language. Dog owners who make an

Dogs use their whole bodies—eyes, ears, tails and voices—to communicate their emotional state. This is a happy dog!

effort can learn to identify their dogs' customary barks. An alarm-bark warning of a stranger's approach sounds different than a "let me in" bark at the door. There's also an excited bark when anticipating an outing, and even an invitation to other dogs to "come on over to my house."

Most domestic canine whining is directed toward humans rather than other canines. And some dogs have sounds all their own. A friend's Puli mix often mumbled in something that sounded like an obscure foreign language. Spirit likes to howl, sometimes very quietly, as if she is consoling herself. Serling does a remarkably accurate pig snort and hums softly when he is content.

Learning your dog's language is one more way to share a little more of his unique world.

A major benefit of the combined senses of the dog is to make hikes in their company far more interesting. And as accomplished

Dogs can help get you up—and keep you on—the trail.

hikers know, an interesting hike is an easier hike. You may find you can cover more miles with your dog along than you can alone.

If your dog is of larger size, there can also be a purely physical benefit. He can help you up those long hills. If you really want him to pull, outfit him with a harness rather than a collar.

Dogs are also excellent at finding a faint and growing fainter trail. If there is one established trail that is used more than other potential routes, a dog can point it out to you if he knows what you want. The word "trail" to my dogs means to stay on the established trail. In instances where I may have some question about just where the established trail actually lies, they have no problem at all. They have led me past rough patches back onto the best trail with great ease, saving possibly miles of bushwhacking.

A dog in camp can also give you an excuse for *not* going on some walks. If dogs are not allowed on the chosen trail, someone has to stay behind to mind the canine.

You will find that having a dog along provides security, companionship and heightened interest.

CHAPTER

6

In Camp

C amping styles vary widely. But whether you backpack a shelter tent and bedroll or drive a forty-foot RV, there will have to be a place for the dog. Regulations have changed over time. When I started camping with dogs, the dogs slept outside the tent, one on the door flap and one at the rear. Hearing their occasional soft growls at imagined dangers they were keeping from the tent was part of the experience. Now, that would be against the rules in most campgrounds: Dogs must be inside the tent or a vehicle at night.

Many campgrounds also limit the number of dogs per campsite. When a friend and I and our four dogs go off on vacation together, we usually have to reserve either a "family" campsite (large enough for several tents) or two regular campsites. If you are a multiple-dog family, this is something to check into when you are making preparations. During camping season in some areas, it is not at all likely that there will be an extra vacant campsite should you need one.

Be aware that some campgrounds, particularly state campgrounds, charge a "dog fee." This seems rather unfair to responsible dog owners, who leave a site as they found it (or better), but it's a fact of life. It's better than being shut out entirely.

One of the greatest rewards of the day: enjoying the campsite with your dog. *Photo courtesy Tim and Wendy Paradis.*

Around the Campfire

Some dogs seem to enjoy a good fire as much as their humans. They will snuggle close to the warmth, curl up and go to sleep. Just how close they come to the fire can be a matter of concern. Some dogs don't seem as sensitive to heat, perhaps because of thick coats, and can end up with singed whiskers or a parched nose. For heavily coated dogs, sparks are also a danger. A spark landing on thick fur will not be felt until it has burned down to the skin. There's nothing like hearing a tired dog grunting contentedly by the fire at night, but it's up to you to be sure that the dog is safe from harm as well as contented.

Cooking fires are perhaps even more hazardous because the dog is attracted to the food. Your attention may also be distracted by going to the vehicle for supplies or looking through boxes for some

Make sure you check your dog for insects and injuries every night at the campsite.

necessary item. Before beginning to cook, be sure your dog is safely and comfortably out of harm's way. This is where a crate or an exercise pen can come in very handy. Tie-outs are fine as long as your dog doesn't insist on tangling herself in the line every two minutes. There is now a retractable tie-out made by the Flexi-Lead Company that can help with that. I know someone who uses an old Flexi-lead tied to a tree a little distance away; it prevents tangles and keeps dirt to a minimum.

I am fully aware of how hectic it can be to try to set up a camp and get food on the table (if there is a table). But slow down! Camping is supposed to be an enjoyable experience, after all. *Do not* let problems and a short temper boil over in the direction of your dog. The dog doesn't know you're angry because someone forgot to pack the can opener, or that the cooler sprang a leak and soaked the sleeping bag. Even if the dog herself is responsible for some mishap, she had to be given the opportunity by her humans. Take a deep breath and relax.

If one of your campfire activities is toasting marshmallows, please do not give them to the dog straight from the fire. Dogs are not always cautious about hot foods and could seriously burn their mouths. If you must give the dog a marshmallow, let it be an untoasted one—even better, give him some jerky or a dog biscuit instead.

When you are sitting around the campfire is an excellent time to feel over your dog to see whether any ticks have attached themselves during the day's hiking, or whether there are burrs tangled deep in the coat. The light may not be great for actually looking for problems, but your dog will enjoy all the touching, and with a coated dog, feeling is more effective than looking anyway. Just gently feel over every inch of skin or use a comb with closely spaced teeth over the whole dog. The comb will remove burrs and tangles and will catch on attached ticks. Don't forget inside the ears, around the jaws, and between the toes. If you do find ticks, use the tweezers from your first-aid kit to remove them, and drown them in a can or bottle filled with water.

If your dog has engaged in swimming or wading, or you have been out in the rain, dry her off when you return to the campsite. Dogs can get chills, and being wet as night falls and the temperature drops can be uncomfortable. Position her close (but not too close) to the fire or other heat, and rub her down with some of those old towels you brought along.

Sometimes serious injuries can be masked by dirt, so it is *essential* that you clean your dog off before bedding down.

My friend and I were walking our four dogs along a stream. It was a sort of trashy area, but the best available at the time, and we tried to steer the dogs around the broken glass and discarded cans and wire. Her dog Starsky let out a yelp, but we saw nothing wrong when we checked him over and he wasn't limping, so we continued our walk. Back in camp I washed the mud off of all canine feet. When Starsky's feet and legs were clean, a narrow spurt of blood began rhythmically pulsing from one leg. A piece of wire had apparently run into his leg and nicked an artery, and the mud had then sealed the wound. I held him on his back in my lap and kept pressure on the injured leg while my friend drove us to the vet, and Starsky was fine after a brief operation. But if we had failed to clean off those muddy feet, he probably would have bled to death before we even realized anything was wrong.

Always be aware that camping is by far the dirtiest way to travel. This is a fact of life, and realizing it will help keep you from being upset about it. Dogs contribute an extra portion of dirt, sometimes to an amazing degree. Brushing them, toweling them off, and putting them directly into the tent or RV will help keep this dirt to a minimum, and also allow you to check for any potential problems.

Some people employ space heaters in their tents. It is extremely important that they be secured so that they cannot be tipped over. The dog's sleeping area should not be too close to the heater.

Any source of heat should be viewed as a potential hazard and treated with caution. Also remember that a couple of dogs in a tent are themselves a heat source. The expression "three dog night" originated as a comment that it was so cold it took three dogs rather than the usual two to keep warm.

Dogs can also prove to be excellent campfire entertainment. They will make games out of the most mundane circumstances. Some people find camping rather boring once the sun has gone down and outside activities are limited. A dog engaged in energetic pursuit of moths hovering around your camp lantern can be a remarkably good substitute for television or reading. Dogs in training, if neither of you is too tired, can practice their lessons in this least distracting of environments.

Food and Water

Your dog should be fed her usual food to avoid possible digestive upsets. (Of course, after the wonderful odor of all that barbecuing food, sharing a piece of cooked hamburger mixed in with the kibble won't hurt.) If possible, keep to your normal feeding schedule. Dogs have an excellent internal clock and are well aware when it is dinnertime.

If the weather will be frosty where you are camping, do not use metal water or food bowls. The dog's tongue could stick to the metal.

Since camping holidays often mean an increased level of activity for all participants, including the dog, it is important to consider when to feed and water the dog. Letting the dog eat or gulp water too soon before or after exercise can result in life-threatening circumstances, most notably bloat and gastric torsion. As a general rule, allow two hours between food and exercise. If your dog gulps water, offer small amounts at spaced intervals rather than letting her drink her fill all at once. Bloat can be fatal in only a couple of hours—if you are really out in the wilderness, you will not even have time to reach a veterinarian.

Try to offer only as much food as your dog will eat. Any leftovers will have to be dealt with. Dog food is a powerful attractant for all sorts of night-roaming critters, most of which you don't want paying you a visit. If you feed dry kibble, you can simply dump any leftovers back into the bag or other container and store it along with your other groceries. But if you feed canned food, putting away leftovers can be a messy proposition. Be sure and bring along a small container just for that purpose.

When you wash your cooking utensils, don't forget the dog bowl.

Do not feed your dog raw hamburger or other uncooked meat or raw eggs. While dogs seem less likely to be affected by *E. coli* (the culprit in human sickness from undercooked burgers at fast-food restaurants), they are fully susceptible to salmonella. Symptoms

---

Understanding and Preventing Bloat

Bloat is technically referred to as gastric dilatation volvulus. Gastric dilatation is distention of the stomach caused by an accumulation of gas or frothy material. In this state, the stomach can rotate (volvulus), closing it off in both directions. The result: compression of one of the major veins carrying blood to the heart, which slows down circulation and leads to shock and death.

Bloat has been widely studied to try to pinpoint its cause and the breeds of dogs that are most prone to it. Breeds apparently most at risk include Great Danes, Weimaraners, Saint Bernards, Gordon Setters, Irish Setters and Standard Poodles. The dog's sex or whether it was neutered or spayed does not appear to matter.

Age may be a factor. Dogs aged seven or older are reported to be twice as likely to get bloat as dogs aged two to four. Also, the more nervous the dog, the more he tends to gulp, and dogs who gulp water are at greater risk. Incidents of bloat are reported most often in the late afternoon and evening and can be associated with stressful or exciting events, like a thunderstorm or trip. Diet does not appear to be a factor, though dogs maintained at their proper weight are healthier in general.

The truth is, bloat can strike any dog without warning. If you notice your dog in discomfort, getting up and down, attempting to vomit with no results, whining and pacing, or with his stomach painful and distended, he may be suffering from bloat. Emergency treatment is necessary to save the dog's life.

---

include severe diarrhea, vomiting, loss of appetite, depression, dehydration and weakness.

Camp Etiquette

Though generalities can be dangerous, campers are a pretty easy-going group. They are used to seeing dogs in campgrounds and

These dogs are all interested in the campers at the next site, but are well-behaved and quiet, sure to be appreciated by everyone.

probably won't object to a little barking. That's a *little* barking, not a half-hour doggy concerto.

To keep everyone happy (and to contribute to a favorable impression and help to keep camping and outdoor recreation open to dogs) requires only some common sense.

Do not let dogs run loose. Aside from any injuries they may inflict on themselves, loose-running dogs can totally disrupt a campground. They are maddening to dogs who are responsibly confined. They can steal food, frighten children (and adults), pee on other people's possessions, leave piles of excrement, chase wildlife, and in general create mayhem. You may find yourself being told to pack up and get out when the dog is traced back to you.

Keep barking under control. It is only natural for a dog in a camp, with all those exciting sights, sounds and smells bombarding her senses, to give in to the urge to vocalize occasionally. A short

Don't let your dog dig. Flat ground is a must for tent campers.

volley of barks (or medly of howls, if your dog is more inclined to "sing" than to "speak") will probably not upset anyone unduly . . . unless it happens to be somewhere around 2 A.M. As long as it is not the middle of the night, let the dog express herself for a moment, then tell her to be quiet. Do not make more noise than the dog, shouting at her to shut up. Remember that teaching the dog to be quiet on command was part of your preparations.

Having the dog near you at night, inside the tent or the recreational vehicle, will solve most of the late-night noise problems. At least if something does set her off, you will be the first one awakened!

Be sure to pick up all droppings deposited by your dog anywhere in the campgrounds, and dispose of them in an appropriate receptacle. No one wants to have to wade through doggy land mines

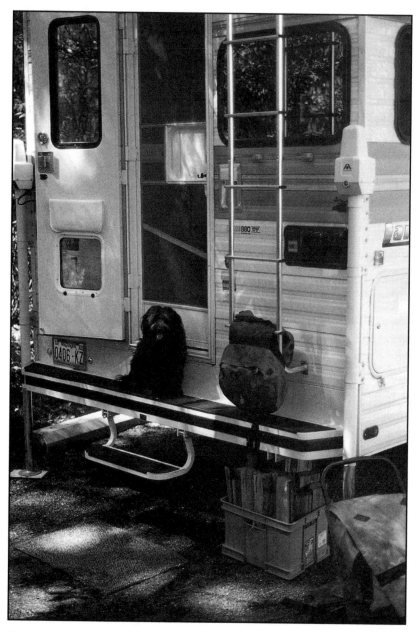

If your dog is used to being left in your RV while you go sightseeing, that's fine, but make sure he's securely inside.

when trying to negotiate the path to the rest rooms by flashlight. Plastic bags, whether small sandwich bags or larger vegetable bags, work perfectly well.

Don't let your dog dig. Level ground is extremely important to campers. If you have always traveled by RV, you may not be aware of how crucial a flat piece of ground is to a tent camper. Take my word for it. No one wants to sleep on rolling mounds of dirt, and no one wants to have to fill in your dog's excavations. If your dog does engage in some digging while your attention is elsewhere, fill in the hole and tamp it as flat as possible.

These are all very minor adjustments to make to ensure that you, your dog and your campground neighbors have a safe and enjoyable camping experience.

Leaving Camp

As an economy measure, some people use a campground as their center of operations to tour the surrounding countryside. Some park the RV and tour in the car they towed behind them; others set up the tent and continue touring in the now-less-crowded automobile. I would hope that the dog is included in these expeditions.

But what if the place you will be visiting does not admit dogs? First, you should know in advance whether this is going to occur, and make plans. Consider the following when making those plans.

If your RV remains in camp while you tour and your dog is used to being there quietly by himself, leaving him in camp may be an option. But only if the weather is not too hot or too cold. Do not depend on the RV's air conditioner or heater to keep the interior temperature controlled. Campground power can be prone to outages. Or, if you are using your own generator, that too could fail. Or the air conditioner or heater itself could go haywire.

It is also a bad idea to leave the RV's solid door open, hoping to let air flow through the screen door. RV screen door latches are notoriously insecure. A good shove from your dog and she could be free and wandering off to look for you.

You can't just expect your dog to wave goodbye and wait quietly in camp while you go off touring all day.

Leaving a dog alone in a tent is rarely a good idea. Most tents today are made of thin plastic fabric, after all, and offer little barrier to a dog determined to get out. Tents, especially with door and window flaps closed, can become extremely humid and unpleasant.

If you will not be gone overly long, the weather is mild, and your dog is used to being left in a crate, crating may be an option. But use caution. To a dog, being left crated in a strange campground can be an entirely different experience from being left crated in her own home. You may want to try driving a short distance away and waiting to hear whether your dog is going to raise a ruckus.

Unless conditions are quite favorable, leaving your dog in camp alone is a risky proposition. This is one of those times when your plans may have to adjust to accommodate the dog. Many major attractions, such as amusement parks, have their own boarding kennels. You may need a reservation if it is a busy time of year. Your dog might not be happy to be left in a strange dog run, but she should be safe and you can visit her periodically throughout the day.

Always check in advance or be prepared to cancel your plans. Do not drive to some attraction, find out there are no kennels, and leave the dog locked in the car in the parking lot for the whole day while you have fun.

If you are including your dog in your travels, most activities should include her. A one-day visit to some "humans-only" attraction will be forgiven as long as your dog is safe and sound at the end of the day.

Night Visitors

Once a campground quiets down for the night, it may become the focus of a different sort of activity. Wildlife in the area has probably learned that there is often food to be had at some of the campsites and might make nightly checks to see what is available. Visitors could range from mice to skunks to raccoons to bears.

Some of these animals will simply search the area for crumbs or for food left out. Others are a bit more aggressive and will rip open coolers or backpacks to get at your supplies.

The only differences with having a dog along, as far as attracting such attention goes, is that you have dog food in addition to your own supplies, and your dog will probably let you know when wildlife is around. Know what animals may be present where you will be camping, and know how to store food safely in their presence.

If your dog growls or barks a warning during the night, do not send her out to protect your camp. She will likely come back reeking of skunk or punctured with porcupine quills. If you want to try to see whatever is investigating your camp, stay in your tent or RV and shine a flashlight out the door or window. After all, you don't want to encounter a skunk or porcupine either!

You may find your dog more vocal than usual at night, especially if she is not an old hand at camping. To her way of thinking, there's plenty to be vocal about. But now is the time to use your "quiet" training. Quiet time in a campground is an extended period: Some campers bed down and get up with the setting and rising of the sun; others sit up late around the campfire and sleep in far into the morning. Neither group will appreciate being awakened by your dog's barking. My dogs quickly learned that growling softly was acceptable but barking was not.

There may be times when barking is absolutely appropriate, and you may have to trust your dog's instincts. Trainer Mandy Book took all her assistants and their dogs out on a group camping expedition. As might be expected, they had many visitors, attracted by the large number of dogs, and the dogs were, of course, well-behaved. But when one group of people walked into the campground saying they wanted to listen to the "singalong" her group was having, the dogs became wildly upset. The people left, and Mandy's group learned the next day that these same visitors went on to another group area and threw rocks through tents and generally raised hell. Somehow the dogs *knew* that these people were different than all the others who had visited. Knowing that dogs can sense these things often gives their owners a warm, fuzzy feeling of security.

CHAPTER 7

More Than a Companion

I n chapter 5, you read about how your dog's senses can help you enjoy the wilderness experience. But there are even more direct ways your dog can make your forays into the backcountry more fun and less of an effort.

Though it probably wasn't the reason behind their domestication, dogs have been serving humans as pack and draft animals for hundreds, possibly thousands, of years. Early explorers of the North American interior reported seeing large Indian tribes on the move. They had no horses—the European introduction of horses to the Americas came later. Instead they had hundreds of dogs, some wearing a rough sort of saddlebag, some pulling travois, some with both pack and travois.

Farther north, where the Nordic breeds developed, a good team of sled dogs was a necessity of life. And in Scandinavia, home of cross-country skiing, the idea of using dog power wasn't long in coming.

Could your family pet become a working member of your outdoor excursions? As long as he is healthy and of reasonable size, there's no reason not to try. Just imagine the dog carrying that rain slicker you thought you might need, and a flashlight in case you're late getting back, and even a change of shoes and socks for those times you slip while crossing on river rocks. Or the luxury of skiing across the landscape without having to propel yourself every step of the way. Not very many people will have an opportunity to use a dog sled as actual transportation, but you just might find yourself addicted to it as a sport.

Dog Packing

This is the easiest and probably most useful way to employ "dog power." A canine health check is especially essential before putting a pack on a dog. As long as your dog doesn't have hip dysplasia, back problems or other structural maladies, even a twenty-pound dog should be able to pull his weight.

Well, actually, a dog can pack only one-quarter to one-third of his weight (depending on which authorities you listen to). But even

Could your pet become a working member of your expeditions? *Photo courtesy Tim and Wendy Paradis.*

on true backpacking expeditions, where you have to pack in food for yourself and your dog, the dog can manage his food and still have some carrying capacity left over for your supplies. This can either lighten your load or allow you to bring luxuries you would otherwise leave behind. Maybe you reluctantly leave that telephoto lens at home, knowing it might net you some great wildlife photos but just not having room for its bulk. Your dog can carry it for you (though you'll want to be sure it's protected in a well-padded case).

You can find dog packs in mail-order catalogs, but fit is important. Unless you are dealing with specialists in dog packing, who can advise you on exactly what measurements they need and how to make them, better to take your dog with you and visit a good sporting goods store or pet supply megastore.

Dogs can overheat easily, so you don't want packs that are going to hold heat against the body. Treated canvas is an excellent breathable material that would be a good choice if you were going to make your own dog pack. But most of the packs offered for sale are made of nylon. Look for as much nylon mesh against the dog as possible, for maximum cooling.

Fit is crucial. You do not want any part of the pack to impede the dog's movement. And you don't want the straps chafing your dog's chest or belly. The pack should ride as far forward as possible—weight over the kidneys is just as uncomfortable for a dog as it is for a horse or a human. A well-fitted pack should hang naturally over the dog's back, not bulge out at both sides.

There is some controversy over how straps should be fastened. Buckles and rings can rub and cause sores. Velcro can get so muddied up that it will no longer hold. To avoid losing your pack and equipment or having to carry it yourself, you should use buckles. But check often to be sure that they are not bothering your dog. Or invest in a cinch cover (meant to slide over the belly band on a horse saddle) and adapt it to your dog pack straps.

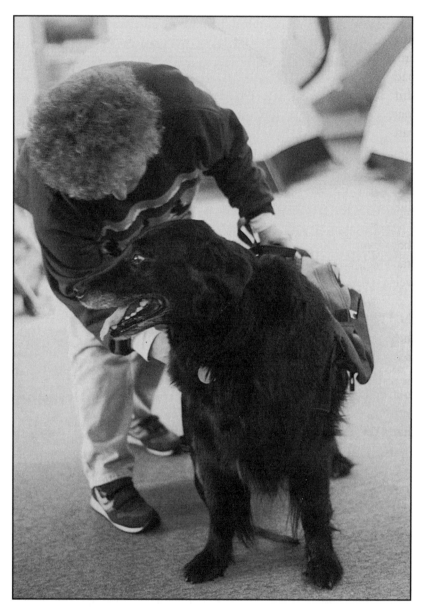

It's important that your dog's backpack fit well. Take your dog with you when you visit the sporting goods store.

While your dog is learning to carry a pack, you can be learning how to load it. The two sides *must* balance. Unlike most other pack animals, dogs do not have the prominent withers that help hold a pack in place. They also have a lively walk or dog trot that will soon shift an unbalanced load. A dog will not be happy with a shifting load, and you will not be happy straightening a pack every hundred yards.

The easiest way to balance a load is to put identical items on each side. If you are bringing a pair of shoes, put one in each pack. If your dog will be carrying his own food, weigh it into zipper bags divided evenly.

Single items offer more of a challenge. What can counterbalance that pair of binoculars? You may want to divide the load into two stacks and weigh each, then make adjustments until the two piles weigh the same.

For your dog's comfort, place soft items first, across the inside of the pack, the surface that will ride against your dog's sides. Arrange the rest so that the bags bulge as little as possible. Pad any sharp items.

How do you get your dog to carry this weight you are learning to arrange? Since you and he have practiced obedience training together, you already have a working relationship. You will rely on that, the dog's common sense, and familiarity.

Load the pack with something moderately bulky and not too heavy—maybe a local phone book on each side. Strap the pack onto your dog. The front strap goes across his chest like a horse's breast collar, securely enough to limit how much the pack can slip back when the dog is going uphill. Keeping the pack forward helps focus the load over the shoulders.

The second strap goes under the dog, just behind the front legs, so that it is crossing the breastbone. It is the canine equivalent of a horse saddle's cinch strap and should *not* go across the belly. A padded cinch cover can ensure that your dog does not suffer sores, and the added width will also help hold the strap in place.

113

With some training, smart packing and experience, your dog should come to love "carrying his weight" on a trip.

Add some of your dog's favorite treats to the pack, clip on your dog's leash, and go for a walk.

If your dog engages in any behavior that would endanger a real load in the pack—banging or rubbing against trees or other objects, rolling, biting at the pack—reprimand him. Otherwise, treat the walk as a fun outing, and offer the dog an occasional treat and praise using a command such as "Good pack." You can also help your dog learn not to bump the pack into his surroundings by having him wear it around the house, puffed out with light items.

A confident, obedience-trained dog should quickly adjust to packing. Many will in fact become protective of their pack and guard it even when not wearing it. After a couple of outings, your dog will know that his pack means exciting travels into the outdoors.

Increase the pack's load gradually. As the date of your planned trip approaches, begin loading the pack with the weight you intend to have your dog carry. Continue taking walks, making them progressively longer, if possible. This also offers an opportunity for you to get in condition.

When you are planning for the actual expedition, remember that your dog's body will be warm against his pack and that he will jostle his load. In the summer, the dog pack can be so hot that it will destroy any perishable food, including cheese, and even damage camera film. Expect that anything you entrust to your dog may be shaken, banged, dirtied, rolled on or submerged.

Keeping your dog on-leash will help prevent such potentially detrimental behavior. In fact, experienced packers say they would not be willing to entrust their possessions to an off-leash dog. But the choice is yours (if leashes aren't mandatory where you will be hiking). There are specific circumstances in which a leash can be either a valuable safety measure or a hindrance.

Near fast-moving water, a leash can keep your dog from such foolhardy beha-vior as leaping in. My dog Serling, who is part Newfoundland, has learned to respect moving water. But in his youth, if it was wet, he was in it, regardless of any possible danger. Though he is a very strong swimmer, the added weight of a soaked pack could be enough of an impediment to change an exciting dip to a total disaster. The control of a leash can keep your dog safe and your possessions dry. And if the dog (or you) should fall in while crossing, the leash can serve as a rescue line.

Mountain climbing is another story. This is not true mountain climbing, with pitons and ropes, but hiking over steep, rocky terrain. Dogs need to be able to pick their own way in these conditions, and a leash may be a handicap, especially if you pull on it while adjusting your own balance. Consider your dog's safety when deciding whether to use a leash.

On a packing expedition, your dog will require a much greater amount of water. A medium-sized dog, around fifty pounds, will need as much water as you, if not more. Remember that lakes and streams are not safe sources of drinking water for either of you. Carry water, or carry some means of water purification. Drink often, and be sure that your dog does the same.

If you are truly backpacking, you will of course need to carry food for your dog. Be aware that your dog will be expending much more energy carrying a pack and will therefore require a greater number of calories. Rather than bringing more food, bring a food more dense in calories. There are several "high-stress" or "performance" dog foods on the market. They will not only provide the calories your dog requires, with less bulk, they will also result in a reduced amount of stools that you will have to clean up along the trail. Begin mixing the high-calorie food with your dog's normal food before leaving home so that your dog will be acclimated to the performance diet.

Dogs have the advantage over horses of being able to sit and lie down while wearing their pack. But if you stop to rest and take off your own pack, take off your dog's, too. It will give him a chance to shake, to cool down and to ease any muscles that may be bothering him. (He won't be able to tell you about them, after all.)

Skijoring

I will admit right at the outset that I have not tried this myself. I use snowshoes rather than cross-country skis, and snowshoes do not lend themselves to dog power. But if your dog is medium-sized or larger, and obedience trained, it should take only a few lessons to transform him into a willing four-legged powerpack to help get you where you want to go.

My most basic piece of advice is that if you are not already an experienced cross-country skier, you should learn the sport yourself before asking your dog to be involved. More good advice is offered by R. Randal Son, who actually participates in this sport and has written about his experiences. "The critical command for your dog to perform is (believe me) 'Whoa!' followed immediately by 'Stay!' When you are in a skis-akimbo pile on the side of the trail, the last thing you need is worried dogs trying to be helpful, adding their lines to your tangle."

Other commands not covered by basic obedience that you will find useful include Hike (go), Gee (turn right), Haw (turn left) and Easy (slow down, steady).

If you are considering trying this sport, you should already have cross-country skiing equipment. Your dog(s) will need a pulling harness and traces. If they are not protected by a heavy coat of their own, they should have a sweater or blanket. The Nordic breeds are naturals for this, but any dog with a strong urge to run will make a skijoring dog. One to three dogs are generally used per person, depending on how much ground you want to cover or how fast you want to go.

You will need a skijoring harness for yourself. This beltlike device attaches the dog(s) to you while leaving your hands free, and keeps the pull from the dogs centered at your pelvis for better balance. You will also need good layers of warm clothing, as the dogs

R. Randal Son skijors with his Huskies, Kai–T and Mischa. *Photo courtesy J. Simon Son.*

will move you through the cold air faster than you would manage under your own power, with less exertion on your part. R. Randal Son notes that the word "skijor" may come from the Norwegian meaning "to plow snow with your face." He's joking, but you do stand an excellent chance of coming in full-body contact with the snow at least once, so you want clothes that will keep you warm even if wet.

To protect against emergencies, carry extra traces and harness snaps in case something breaks when you are many miles from civilization. Consider how you would respond if your dog sprains or breaks a leg. Spare ski poles and a blanket are not much to carry, and can be rigged to make a travois for transporting an injured dog.

Though skijoring is gaining in popularity, it is far from common. Most cross-country skiers are not used to encountering dogs on the trail. Demonstrating good control and thoughtfulness in picking up after your dogs will result in a good image for this rising sport.

R. Randal Son offers a final comment. "Skijoring is exhilarating, frustrating, hilarious, peaceful, occasionally panic-inspiring, and tremendous fun for you and your dogs. Hike!"

Dog Carting and Sledding

I am partially qualified to speak about this use of dog power. While I have not dog sledded, I have dog carted. Though the two activities employ different vehicles, the dog training and commands necessary for control are much the same.

You can start with a pup as young as two months. Put a soft harness on him, and let him drag a small log around. Older dogs can learn, too. Serling was seven when he was introduced to carting. He was in the process of earning his CDX (Companion Dog Excellent, a mid-level obedience title), so obedience was not a problem. And he didn't object to wearing a harness. He had walked beside our dolly cart for years. (For those of you who've never been involved in any sort of dog showing, a flat wheeled cart on which to stack the

Dog sledding is a popular wintertime activity for people with enough dogs and the right equipment. *Photo courtesy R. Randal Son.*

exercise pen, chairs, and all the other equipment you accumulate is just about essential.) Since he was already familiar with the load I wanted him to haul, I just hooked him up one day, using ten-foot traces. He may have been a little surprised, but he leaned into the harness and pulled willingly. We were the envy of all the other exhibitors, who were pulling their own carts up the hill to the show grounds.

Serling has always been the "class clown" of dogdom, and once he realized that it got him attention, he loved pulling. We started giving rides on his dolly cart to other exhibitors between classes. They, of course, fussed over him to no end.

A dolly cart is not an easy thing to ride (being about three inches off the ground), so we bought a dog cart. This is a cut-down version of a horse's harness-racing sulky, with a seat, two wheels and two shafts. It was a lot more comfortable for passengers, and we could still strap equipment across the seat and use it in place of the dolly cart.

Up to this point, I had been running alongside Serling and guiding him. Now I wanted to ride myself. I had to teach him to drive. This was by far the hardest part. I had unwittingly trained Serling that when he pulled, I was beside him. Now I had to break that training.

I started out with him wearing his training collar and leash while in harness and pulling the empty cart. We would go out for a walk, and I would gradually drop back until I was walking behind the cart. Serling already knew "walk on" (keep going straight ahead), "easy" (an *essential* command, since his natural speed when in harness could run down a cheetah), and "whoa." Now I started using "left" and "right" as I used the leash, to guide him into turning.

It was weeks before I could sit tentatively in the cart. Then we had interesting outings with Serling turning the cart in tight little circles as he tried to turn around and come to me. He was always happier with someone else in the cart and me walking alongside.

Though I thought about taking him up to the Sierra when one of the dog sledding clubs was holding races, we never got there. He's retired now, but I think he would have enjoyed pulling on snow.

If you are interested in carting (not likely to be of much use in the backcountry), the nearest Newfoundland, St. Bernard or Bernese Mountain Dog breed clubs may be able to help you. These breeds all compete in carting trials. The Newfoundland parent club offers some publications that may be of interest (they are listed in Appendix B).

For sledding, there are two groups: the ISDRA (International Sled Dog Racing Association) and the IWPA (International Weight Pulling Association). Both have been pleasant and helpful whenever I have contacted them. They are also listed in Appendix B.

And of course there are always books. Several of these are listed in Appendix B, too, but you could find more at your library or through one of the breed clubs.

CHAPTER 8

Walking Lightly on the Land

Throughout this book, I have been harping on responsibility. Though you may think I have gone overboard, nothing could be more important. Not only do you have the usual backcountry obligation to "leave only footprints, take only photographs," but having a dog along forces a deeper level of commitment. You are responsible for the well-being of your furry friend, and you are a representative of dog owners everywhere—whether you want to be or not.

I'm sure you are totally disgusted when you arrive at some mountain lake to find that a slob or group of slobs has decorated the landscape with beer cans and candy wrappers. Though hundreds of people may have hiked to this spot, it takes only one uncaring person to ruin the experience for everyone else. Well, other people feel exactly the same about any dog droppings left littering the landscape. And don't mistakenly think that they are all dog haters; some of the most upset will be other dog owners, who *have* picked up after their pets.

Many land managers see dogs as a potential nuisance and are willing to ban them from areas at the slightest provocation. It is up to you to give them no reason for doing so.

"Leave only footprints, take only photographs." Litterbugs are not welcome!

Leaving Wildlife in Peace

Contrary to the assertions of some land managers, the presence of a dog does not automatically cause all wildlife to vacate the vicinity. In fact, I see more wildlife with my dog by my side than I ever do on my own, thanks to the dog's superior senses. And the wild things are not fleeing in panic. In fact, deer have often approached us with obvious curiosity. Squirrels move only far enough to feel safe, then stop to taunt us with relish. In the company of dogs, I have seen pica, marmot, hare, porcupine, coyote, fox, pronghorn, bighorn, deer, elk, moose, bear, water birds of every kind, hawks and eagles. Only the hares disappeared with any haste.

Dogs should relieve themselves well away from a source of water so that there is no danger of fouling it.

But any incident that is even perceived as wildlife harassment is a very black mark. It is used to close more areas to dogs, and it can create massive domino effects. Unless your dog is trustworthy, and will come *every* time you call, regardless of the circumstances, do not even think about letting her go off-leash. If you do choose to relinquish the control of a leash, you must be much more alert

125

to potential problems. You cannot become engrossed in conversation with your hiking companion and forget about the dog.

For most family dogs, a camping or hiking holiday provides much more activity than the daily routine does. Running off-leash may be fun and exciting, but she will get plenty of exercise staying closer to your side, and she will not have the opportunity to get skunked, snakebitten or otherwise injured.

Dealing with Dog Excrement

No one wants to have to watch where they are putting their feet rather than the scenery. And certainly no one wants to step in a pile of dog feces. Dog excrement is another prime reason cited for banning dogs not just from wilderness areas, but from city parks as well.

There are varying strategies for countering this problem. Some long-time hikers maintain that simply removing the offending matter from the trail is enough. I don't agree. Just seeing a piece of dog poop is enough to offend some people, and with ever-increasing visitation to wilderness areas there would soon be plenty to see if no one picked up.

So whatever your dog deposits, you need to pick up. If you are hiking in a relatively developed area where trash cans are available, all it takes is a plastic bag. Pick up your dog's pile, and carry it along to the nearest trash can. But most trails do not have trash receptacles conveniently placed along them. So what do you do?

You can still use a plastic bag to pick up the offending material. Then you can drop bag and all into a zipper-locked plastic bag and seal it up. With the mess and odor locked safely away, you can slip it into your dog's pack, your own pack, or a jacket pocket, and pack it out as you should all garbage.

For people who just can't deal with carrying excrement, no matter how many bags contain it, there is the cat-hole option. Backcountry campers will be familiar with this waste-disposal strategy. Dig a narrow hole about six inches deep. Place the feces in it and cover with dirt and leaves.

No one finds this subject pleasant, but dog owners *must* clean up or face being barred from more and more areas. If you want to be able to hike and camp with your furry friend, please make the effort and leave no sign of your passing.

Protecting Water and Wild Areas

Though wild water is, sadly, no longer safe to drink without being treated, that doesn't mean we shouldn't work to protect it. All campers should follow the rules to wash and rinse dishes and hands at least 200 feet away from any lake or stream. Campers and/or hikers with dogs should also see to it that their dogs relieve themselves at least that same distance from any water source. (This is the rule with *all* companion animals in the backcountry, and if you think it's difficult to convince a dog to wait to whizz, try it with a llama!)

There is a more obscure problem that you can do your part to help prevent. Foreign plants are invading wild areas, often overrunning more fragile native growth. See to it that you are not part of spreading this problem. Brush your dog before leaving home and after each day's outings to be sure that she is not carrying weed seeds in her coat. Check your outer clothing as well.

Trash

As people have become more environmentally aware, overpackaging and therefore potential trash have decreased a bit. But only a bit. The best way to deal with this problem that besets wilderness areas everywhere is to think about it before leaving home.

Whether I'm camping or just hiking, most of my supplies are repackaged into either zipper bags or aluminum foil before they leave the house. The aluminum foil squashes down nicely once empty and can be recycled back home. The zipper bags become part of my

Trails can be enjoyed by people and dogs of all ages. It is up to us to demonstrate that our dogs should be allowed.

dog-waste-removal system once their contents are consumed. They are also excellent specimen bags if you are in an area where it is appropriate to collect shells or other natural objects.

When you are planning your own expedition, consider how you can best decrease your trash burden.

Opening More Areas

It is a little-known fact that there is no national policy regarding allowing dogs in or banning dogs from national parks or national forests. Each manager has the authority to decide on policy for his or her specific area. Unfortunately, most choose to ban dogs rather than have to deal with any number of irresponsible dog owners.

Believe me, I am an ardent supporter of our national parks and forests. I know how badly paid and understaffed park rangers are. But I am tired of dog owners being singled out as a group. A few slobs throw trash or even burning cigarettes from cars, but drivers are not banned. Children pick flowers or throw junk food to wild animals, but children aren't banned. Why? Because people would scream in outrage at any attempt to ban cars or kids. Dog owners have not been so vocal. Now seems to be the time to start speaking up or face being barred from more and more of your public lands.

People who object to dogs in parks or on trails are very outspoken. They complain, they write letters. The land managers hear only this side of the story and react by banning dogs. It is time they heard the other side of the story—not shrilly, but in well-reasoned fashion. Do you hike on your own and feel more secure because you have your dog for company? I often do, and that's a valid reason for requesting dog access. Dogs need exercise, too, of course, and a soft dirt trail through natural areas is far preferable to pavement at the side of a road. But one very large reason that many people seem to overlook is that these are *public* lands and *we* are the public. If we demonstrate responsibility and lack of impact, there is no reason we should be barred. Tell your local land management official why you

Tell your local land management official why you love to hike with your dog.

love to hike with your dog and why you want to secure the privilege for all who share your pleasure. See Appendix A for addresses and phone numbers.

Canine Courtesy

"Imagine yourself in a room with several other people. You are standing visiting, minding your own business, perhaps engrossed in conversation or listening. Suddenly, the door bursts open and in runs another person. This person runs around to everyone and slaps them on the back, bumping into everyone in the process. Some people are kissed sloppily, some are hit with both hands on the chest in greeting. What would your reaction be?"

Carol Monroe wrote those words for a magazine article a few years ago, and they still make their point. Uncontrolled dogs can be an annoyance to humans and other dogs.

Just because your dog happens to be friendly and exuberant, don't expect all dogs to welcome being sniffed, pawed at, or broadsided. People may be even less tolerant of such behavior. Some people simply find dogs repulsive or terrifying, and that's their right.

To justify the continued presence of dogs in public areas, we need to demonstrate responsibility and good manners at all times and see that our dogs do the same.

After the Trip

This is a very short chapter to offer you two important pieces of advice. First, you have worked to get your dog into shape and he is now used to a certain amount of exercise and to listening to your commands. Don't let your work go to waste just because you're home. You don't want to have to start at ground zero again to get ready for your *next* trip, do you?

Keep up the exercise. It's good for your dog and for you. It keeps him content and less likely to get into trouble. And it is quality time for the two of you to spend together.

Don't forget the obedience either. The ability to command your dog to sit and wait until you say it's all right to go through an open door can be a lifesaver in any location. Asking the dog to do a down-stay while you eat dinner eliminates begging at the table. Taking a walk without having your arm pulled from its socket is also a benefit. Obedience is meant to be used in everyday life.

Keep your dogs in shape between hikes so that they're ready for the next adventure. *Photo courtesy Kimberley Peterson.*

If your dog should develop any health problems after your trip, even weeks or months after, it is crucial that you tell your veterinarian where you have been and any details that might be noteworthy. Did your dog pick up some ticks? Have a close encounter with a ground squirrel? Drink lots of lake water? Some diseases and parasites take quite some time to show symptoms, and many show similar symptoms. The more information you can provide, the easier it will be to make an accurate diagnosis.

Keep up your dog's training between hikes, too. Obedience is for every day.

Finally, while coming home after a trip is always nice, there's usually a letdown of sorts after all the planning and excitement. If you find yourself a bit blue, there's a simple solution—start planning the next outing! And be sure to include your wonderful canine companion.

Sources for Information on Parks and Other Open Space

National Parks

National Park Service
Public Affairs and Tourism
1100 Ohio Dr. SW
Washington, DC 20242
202-619-7222

Western Region
National Park Service
600 Harrison St.
Suite 600
San Francisco, CA 94107-1372
415-556-0560

Southeast Region
National Park Service
75 Spring St., SW
Atlanta, GA 30303-3378
404-331-5187

Midwest Region
National Park Service
1709 Jackson St.
Omaha, NE 68102-2571
402-221-3471

Rocky Mountain Region
National Park Service
P.O. Box 25287
Denver, CO 80225-0287
303-969-2000

Southwest Region
National Park Service
P.O. Box 728
Santa Fe, NM 87504-0728
505-988-6012

Pacific Northwest Region
National Park Service
909 First Ave.
Seattle, WA 98104-1060
206-220-7450

North Atlantic Region
National Service
15 State St.
Boston, MA 02109-3572
617-223-5199

National Capitol Region
National Park Service
1100 Ohio Dr., SW
Washington, DC 20242-0001
202-619-7222

Mid-Atlantic Region
National Park Service
143 S. Third St.
Philadelphia, PA 19106-7018
215-597-7018

Alaska Region
National Park Service
2525 Gambell St.
Anchorage, AK 99503-2892
907-271-2737

National Forests
U. S. Forest Service
Nature of the Northwest
800 N.E. Oregon St.
Suite 177
Portland, OR 97232
503-872-2750 (for general
information, regional maps,
wilderness maps, and books
on hiking and camping)

800-280-2267 (Call to make
reservations. You need to know
the name of the campground at
which you'll be staying and have
a credit card to make the
reservation.)

Pacific Southwest Region
U.S.D.A. Forest Service
630 Sansome St.
San Francisco, CA 94111
415-705-2870
(covers California only)

Southern Region
U.S.D.A. Forest Service
1720 Peachtree Rd., NW
Atlanta, GA 30367
404-347-2384 (covers Alabama,
Arkansas, Florida, Georgia,
Kentucky, Louisiana, Mississippi,
North Carolina, Oklahoma,
Puerto Rico, South Carolina,
Tennessee, Texas, Virginia, the
Virgin Islands)

Eastern Region
U.S.D.A. Forest Service
310 W. Winconsin Ave.
Milwaukee, WI 53203
414-297-3693 (covers Illinois,
Indiana, Iowa, Michigan,
Minnesota, Missouri, New
Hampshire, Ohio, Pennsylvania,
Vermont, West Virginia,
Wisconsin)

Rocky Mountain Region
U.S.D.A. Forest Service
740 Simms St.
P.O. Box 25127
Lakewood, CO 80225
303-275-5350 (covers Colorado,
Kansas, Nebraska, southwest South
Dakota, eastern Wyoming)

Southwestern Region

U.S.D.A. Forest Service
Office of Information
517 Gold Ave., SW
Albuquerque, NM 87102
505-842-3292 (covers Arizona,
New Mexico)

Northern Region

U.S.D.A. Forest Service
Federal Building
P.O. Box 7669
Missoula, MT 59807-7669
406-329-3511 (covers northern
Idaho, Montana, North Dakota,
northwest South Dakota)

Intermountain Region

U.S.D.A. Forest Service
Federal Building
324 25th St.
Ogden, UT 84401
801-625-5352 (covers southern
Idaho, Nevada, Utah, western
Wyoming)

Pacific Northwest Region

Alaska Region
U.S.D.A. Forest Service
P.O. Box 21628
Juneau, AK 99802-1628
907-586-8863 (covers Alaska)

U.S.D.A. Forest Service
333 S.W. 1st Ave.
P.O. Box 3623
Portland, OR 97208
503-326-2971
(covers Oregon, Washington)

Bureau of Land Management

Alaska Division

U.S. Department of the Interior
Bureau of Land Management
222 W. 7th Ave., #13
Anchorage, AK 99513-7599
907-271-5076

Arizona Division

U.S. Department of the Interior
Bureau of Land Management
3707 N. 7th St.
P.O. Box 16563
Phoenix, AZ 85011
602-650-0500

California Division

U.S. Department of the Interior
Bureau of Land Management
2800 Cottage Way, E-2841
Sacramento, CA 95825
916-979-2845

Colorado Division

U.S. Department of the Interior
Bureau of Land Management
2850 Youngfield St.
Lakewood, CO 80215-7076
303-239-3700

Eastern States Division

U.S. Department of the Interior
Bureau of Land Management
7450 Boston Blvd.
Springfield, VA 22153
703-440-1700

Idaho Division
U.S. Department of the Interior
Bureau of Land Management
3380 Americana Terr.
Boise, ID 83706
208-384-3001

Montana Division
U.S. Department of the Interior
Bureau of Land Management
222 N. 32nd St.
P.O. Box 36800
Billings, MT 59107-6800
406-255-2904

Nevada Division
U.S. Department of the Interior
Bureau of Land Management
850 Harvard Way
Reno, NV 89520-0006
702-785-6590

New Mexico Division
U.S. Department of the Interior
Bureau of Land Management
1474 Rodeo Dr.
P.O. Box 27115
Santa Fe, NM 87502-0115
505-438-7501

Oregon Division
U.S. Department of the Interior
Bureau of Land Management
1515 S.W. 5th Ave.
P.O. Box 2965
Portland, OR 97208-2965
503-952-6024

Utah Division
U.S. Department of the Interior
Bureau of Land Management
324 S. State St.
P.O. Box 45155
Salt Lake City, UT 84145-0155
801-539-4021

Wyoming Division
U.S. Department of the Interior
Bureau of Land Management
2515 Warren Ave.
P.O. Box 1828
Cheyenne, WY 82003
307-775-6001

Service Center
U.S. Department of the Interior
Bureau of Land Management
Denver Federal Center, Building 50
P.O. Box 25047
Denver, CO 80225-0047
303-236-6452

National Interagency Fire Center
U.S. Department of the Interior
Bureau of Land Management
3833 S. Development Ave.
Boise, ID 83705-5354
208-387-5446

National Training Center
U.S. Department of the Interior
Bureau of Land Management
9828 N. 31st Ave.
Phoenix, AZ 85051
602-906-5500

General National

National Parks and Conservation
Association
1776 Massachusetts Ave., NW
Suite 200
Washington, DC 20036
800-628-7275

Point Reyes National Seashore
Point Reyes, CA 94956
415-663-1092

State Parks and Offices of Tourism

(in alphabetical order)

Alabama

Alabama Department of Conservation
Division of State Parks
Administrative Building
64 N. Union St.
Montgomery, AL 36130
334-242-3151

Alabama Tourism & Travel
P.O. Box 4927
Montgomery, AL 36103-4927
800-ALABAMA (800-252-2262)

Alaska

Alaska Division of Tourism
P.O. Box 110801
Juneau, AK 99811-0801
907-465-2010

Arizona

Arizona Office of Tourism
1100 W. Washington
Phoenix, AZ 85007
602-542-8687 (for general touring
information)

Arizona State Parks
1300 W. Washington
Phoenix, AZ 85007
602-542-4174 (for state parks
information)

Arkansas

Arkansas Travel Office
800-NATURAL (800-628-8725)
Department of Parks and Tourism
One Capitol Mall
Little Rock, AR 72201
800-643-8383

California

California Tourist Information
800-TO-CALIF (800-862-2543)

Department of Parks and Recreation
P.O. Box 942896
Sacramento, CA 94296-0001
916-653-6995 or 800-444-7275

MISTIX (for state park campground
reservations)
P.O. Box 85705
San Diego, CA 92186-5705
619-452-1950 (for reservations)
619-452-0150 (for information)

Pacific Gas & Electric
800-743-5000 (for reservations)
916-386-5164 (for group
information)
415-973-5552
(for general information)

Colorado

Colorado Tourism
3554 N. Academy Blvd.
Colorado Springs, CO 80917
800 COLORADO (800-265-6723)
(for information on points of
interest)

Division of Parks and Recreation
1313 Sherman St.
Room 618
Denver, CO 80203
303-866-3437

Connecticut

Connecticut State Parks
79 Elm St.
Hartford, CT 06106-5127
203-566-2304 (recording Mon–Fri)

Connecticut Travel Office
865 Brook St.
Rocky Hill, CT 06067
800-CT BOUND (800-282-6863)

Delaware

Delaware Travel Office
99 Kings Hwy.
P.O. Box 1401
Dover, DE 19903
800-441-8846

District of Columbia

Washington D.C. Travel & Tourism
1212 New York Ave., NW
Suite 600
Washington, DC 20005
202-789-7000

Florida

Florida Park Service
3900 Commonwealth Blvd.
MS 535
Tallahassee, FL 32399-3000
904-488-7326 (for information
on state parks and points of
interest)

Florida Travel Office
904-487-1462

Georgia

Tourist Division
Georgia Department of Industry,
Trade & Tourism
P.O. Box 1776
Atlanta, GA 30301
800-VISIT-GA; 800-847-4842
(for information on points of
interest)

Idaho

Idaho Travel Council
700 W. State St.
P.O. Box 83720
Boise, ID 83720-0093
800-635-7820

Illinois

Illinois Bureau of Tourism
James R. Thompson Center
100 W. Randolph St.
Suite 3-400
Chicago, IL 60601
800-233-0121

Illinois Department of
Conservation
Bureau of Land and Historic Sites
524 S. Second
Lincoln Tower Plaza
Springfield, IL 62702
217-785-8552 (for information
on sites of interest)

Illinois Division of Land
Management
600 N. Grand West
Springfield, IL 62706
217-782-6752 (for information on
state parks)

Indiana

Department of Natural Resources
Division of State Parks
402 W. Washington St.
Room 298
Indianapolis, IN 46204
317-232-4125

Indiana Travel Office
101 N. Governor
Evansville, IN 47711
800-289-6646

Iowa

Iowa Natural Resources
Henry A. Wallace Building
Des Moines, IA 50319-0034
515-281-5145 (for state parks
information)

Iowa Travel Office
2 Ruan Center
601 Locust
Suite 222
Des Moines, IA 50309
800-345-IOWA (800-345-4692)

Kansas

Kansas Travel Office
Kansas Dept. of Commerce
Div. of Travel & Tourism
Development
700 Harrison
Suite 1300
Topeka, KS 66603
800-2KANSAS; 800-252-6727

Parks and Resources Authority
900 Jackson
Room 502
Topeka, KS 66612
913-296-2281

Kentucky

Dept. of Travel Development
Capital Plaza Tower
500 Mero St.
22nd Floor
Frankfort, KY 40601
800-225-TRIP (for travel
information)

Kentucky Dept. of Parks
Capital Plaza Tower
500 Mero St.
10th Floor
Frankfort, KY 40601
800-225-PARK (for state park
campground reservations)

Louisiana

Louisiana Office of State Parks
P.O. Box 44426
Baton Rouge, LA 70804-4426
504-342-8111

Louisiana Office of Tourism
800-633-6970 (for information on
points of interest)

Maine

Maine Travel Office
P.O. Box 2300
Hallowell, ME 04347
207-623-0363 or 800-533-9595
(for state parks and points of
interest)

Maryland

Maryland Travel Office
217 E. Redwood St.
9th Floor
Baltimore, MD 21202
800-543-1036

State Forest and Parks Service
Tawes State Office Bldg. E-3
Annapolis, MD 21401
410-974-3771

Massachusetts

Dept. of Environment
Everett Saltonstall Bldg.
100 Cambridge St.
Government Center
Boston, MA 02202
617-727-3180 (for information on
state parks)

Massachusetts Travel Office
100 Cambridge St.
13th Floor
Boston, MA 02202
617-727-3201 (for tourist
information)

Michigan

Michigan Parks & Recreation
Division
Department of Natural Resources
P.O. Box 30257

Lansing, MI 48909
517-373-9900 or 517-373-1270
(for information on state parks)

Michigan Travel Office
P.O. Box 3393
Livonia, MI 48151-3393
800-543-2937

Minnesota

Minnesota State Parks
800-246-2267 or 612-922-9000
(for camping information)

Minnesota Travel & Tourism
121 7th Place E.
100 Metro Square
St. Paul, MN 55101-2112
800-657-3700 or 612-296-5029

Mississippi

Department of Natural Resources
Bureau of Recreation and Parks
Box 10600
Jackson, MS 39209
601-961-5099

Travel and Tourism Department
Mississippi Department of
Economic Development
P.O. Box 22825
Jackson, MS 39205
800-648-3057 (for information on
points of interest)

Missouri

Missouri Department of Natural
Resources & State Parks
P.O. Box 176
Jefferson City, MO 65102
800-334-6946 or 314-751-2479

Missouri Travel Office
800-877-1234

Montana
Montana Parks
Capital Station
P.O. Box 200701
Helena, MT 59620-0701
406-444-3750

Travel Montana
1424 9th Ave.
Helena, MT 59620
800-548-3390 or 800-541-1447
(for information on points of
interest)

Nebraska
Nebraska Game and Parks
Commission
P.O. Box 30370
Lincoln, NE 68503
402-464-0641

Nebraska Travel & Tourism
P.O. Box 98913
Lincoln, NE 68509
800-228-4307

Nevada
Nevada Commission on Tourism
Capitol Complex
Carson City, NV 89710
800-NEVADA-8; 800-638-2328
(for information on points of
interest)

Nevada Division of State Parks
Capitol Complex
Carson City, NV 89710
702-687-4387

New Hampshire
Division of Parks & Recreation
P.O. Box 1856
Concord, NH 03302
603-271-3556

New Hampshire Travel Office
P.O. Box 1856
Concord, NH 03302-1856
603-271-2666

New Jersey
New Jersey Travel & Tourism
200 W. State St.
Trenton, NJ 08625-0826
609-292-2470

Parks & Forest
501 E. State St.
Trenton, NJ 08625-0826
609-292-2797

New Mexico
New Mexico Travel & Tourism
491 Old Santa Fe Trail
Lamy Building
Santa Fe, NM 87503
800-545-2040 (for information on
points of interest)

State Park and Recreation Division
P.O. Box 1147
Santa Fe, NM 87504
505-827-7465

New York
Natural Resources
50 Wolf Rd.
Albany, NY 12233
518-457-7435

New York Travel Information
Division of Tourism
1 Commerce Plaza
Albany, NY 12245
800-CALL-NYS; 800-225-5697

State Parks Information
Empire State Plaza
Agency Building No. 1
Albany, NY 12238
518-474-0456

North Carolina

Division of Parks and Recreation
Department of Natural Resources
and Community Development
P.O. Box 27687
Raleigh, NC 27611
919-733-4181

North Carolina Division of Travel
and Tourism
430 N. Salisbury St.
Raleigh, NC 27611
800-VISIT NC; 800-847-4862 (for
information on points of interest)

North Dakota

North Dakota State Parks and
Recreation Department
1835 Bismarck Expressway
Bismarck, ND 58504
701-328-5357

North Dakota Tourism
Liberty Memorial Building
604 E. Blvd.
Bismarck, ND 58505
800-437-2077 (for information on
points of interest)

Ohio

Division of Travel & Tourism
P.O. Box 1001
Columbus, OH 43216-1001
800-BUCKEYE; 800-282-5393

Ohio Travel Office
Family Vacation Services
600 W. Spring St.
Columbus, OH 43215 or

TW Recreational Services
P.O. Box 550
Cambridge, OH 43725
614-265-7000 (for state park
information)

800-AT-A-PARK; 800-282-7275
(for reservations at eight state parks)

Oklahoma

Oklahoma Tourism and Recreation
Department Literature Distribution
Center
215 N.E. 28th St.
Oklahoma City, OK 73105
800-652-6552 (for information on
state parks and points of interest)

Oregon

Oregon Parks and Recreation
Department
3554 S.E. 82nd Ave.
Portland, OR 97266
800-452-5687

Oregon Tourism Department
775 Summer St., NE
Salem, OR 97310
800-547-7842

Pennsylvania

Bureau of State Parks
P.O. Box 8551
Harrisburg, PA 17105-8551
800-63-PARKS or 717-787-6640

Pennsylvania Travel Office
800-VISIT-PA; 800-847-4872

Rhode Island

Parks and Recreation
2321 Hartford Ave.
Johnston, RI 02919
401-277-2632 (for campground
information)

Rhode Island Travel Office
7 Jackson Walkway
Providence, RI 02903
800-556-2484

South Carolina

South Carolina Department of
Parks, Recreation and Tourism
Division of State Parks
1205 Pendleton St.
Columbia, SC 29201
803-734-0156 (for information on
state parks and points of interest)

South Carolina Department of
Parks, Recreation and Tourism
1205 Pendleton St.
Suite 106
Columbia, SC 29201
803-734-0235 (for general
information)

South Dakota

Division of Tourism
Capitol Lake Plaza
711 E. Wells Ave.
Pierre, SD 57501
800-732-5682 (for information on
points of interest)

Game, Fish and Parks
Division of Parks and Recreation
Foss Building
523 E. Capitol Ave.
Pierre, SD 57501-3182
605-773-3391

Tennessee

Department of Conservation
Division of State Parks
401 Church St.
L & C Tower, 7th Floor
Nashville, TN 37243-0446
800-421-6683 (for state park
information and campground
reservations)

Tennessee Tourist Development
P.O. Box 23170
Nashville, TN 37202
615-741-2158 (for information on
points of interest)

Texas

Texas Parks and Wildlife
Department
4200 Smith School Rd.
Austin, TX 78744
800-792-1112
512-389-8900 (for reservations)

Texas Travel Office
800-8888-TEX

Utah

Utah Division of Parks
& Recreation
1636 W. North Temple
Salt Lake City, UT 84116-3156
801-538-7221

Utah Travel Council
Council Hall, Capitol Hill
Salt Lake City, UT 84114-7420
800-200-1160 (for information on
points of interest)

Utah Travel Council
801-538-1030

Vermont

Dept. of Parks & Recreation
Montpelier, VT 05602
802-828-3375

Vermont Travel Office
134 State St.
Montpelier, VT 05602
802-828-3236 or 802-828-3237

Virginia
State Parks
203 Governor St.
Richmond, VA 23219
804-786-1712

Virginia Division of Tourism
901 E. Bird St.
19th Floor
Richmond, VA 23219
800-VISIT-VA; 800-847-4882;
or 804-786-4484

Washington
Washington State Department of
Fish and Wildlife
360-902-2200

Washington State Department of
Natural Resources
360-902-1234

Washington State Ferries
206-84-FERRY (800-843-3779)

Washington State Parks and
Recreation
7150 Clearwater Ln.
P.O. Box 42662
Olympia, WA 98504
360-902-8563

Washington State Tourism
Development Division
P.O. Box 42500
Olympia, WA 98504
800-544-1800

West Virginia
Div. of Parks & Recreation
Capitol Complex
Building 6, Room B-451
1900 Kanawha Blvd., E.
Charleston, WV 25305-0317
304-558-2764

West Virginia Travel Office
Telemarketing State Capitol
Complex
Building 6, Room B-564
1900 Kanawha Blvd., E.
Charleston, WV 25305-0317
800-225-5982

Wisconsin
Wisconsin Department of Natural
Resources
Bureau of Parks and Recreation
Box 7921
Madison, WI 53707
608-266-2181

Wisconsin Travel Office
P.O. Box 55
Dodgeville, WI 53595
800-432-TRIP

Wyoming
Wyoming State Parks & Historic
Sites
2301 Central Ave.
Cheyenne, WY 82002
307-777-6323

Wyoming Travel Commission
I-25 College Drive
Cheyenne, WY 82002
800-225-5996 (for information on
points of interest)

CANADA
Alberta Tourism, Parks and
Recreation
P.O. Box 2500
Edmonton, Alberta T5J 2Z4
800-661-8888

Appearance

Appendix A

British Columbia Ministry of
Tourism
Parliament Building
Victoria, BC V8V 1X4
800-663-6000

Travel Manitoba
Dept. 1035, 7th Floor
155 Carlton St.
Winnipeg, Manitoba R3C 3H8
800-665-0040

Tourism New Brunswick
P.O. Box 12345
Fredericton, New Brunswick
E3B 5C3
800-561-0123

Newfoundland and Labrador
Department of Tourism & Culture
P.O. Box 8730
St. John's, Newfoundland A1B 4K2
800-563-6353

Tourism Nova Scotia
The World Trade and
Convention Center
1800 Argyle St.
Halifax, Nova Scotia B3J 2R7
800-341-6096

Ontario Travel
Ministry of Culture, Tourism &
Recreation
Customer Sales and Service
77 Bloor St., W.,
9th Floor Queens Park
Toronto, Ontario M7A 2R9
800-668-2746

Prince Edward Island
Visitor Services
P.O. Box 940
Charlottetown, PEI C1A 7M5
800-565-0267

Tourisme Quebec
CP 979
Montreal, Quebec H3C 2W3
800-363-7777

Tourism Saskatchewan
Saskatchewan Trade &
Convention Centre
1919 Saskatchewan Dr.
Regina, SK S4P 3V7
800-667-7191

Northwest Territories
Travel Arctic, Economic
Development & Tourism
GNWT, P.O. Box 1320
Yellowknife, NW X1A 2L9
800-661-0788

Yukon Territories
Tourism Yukon
P.O. Box 2703
Whitehorse, YT Y1A 2C6
403-667-5340
(in Canada, 800-661-0494)

Other Contacts and Materials to Help with Your Trip

Campground Organizations

American Heritage Campground
9610 Kimme St., SW
Olympia, WA 98512
800-943-8778

Coast to Coast Resorts
64 Inverness Drive, East
Englewood, CO 80112
800-368-5721 (member services)

KOA Campgrounds
P.O. Box 30558
Billings, MT 59114
800-548-7239

Thousand Trails & NACO
2711 LBJ Freeway
Dallas, TX 75234
800-285-3594

RV Organizations

Family Motor Coach Association
8291 Clough Pike
Cincinnati, OH 45244

Canine Organizations

American Kennel Club
51 Madison Ave.
New York, NY 10010
212-696-8204

Bernese Mountain Dog Club of America
Ms. Roxanne Bortnick, Secretary
P.O. Box 270692
Fort Collins, CO 80527

International Sled Dog Racing Association, Inc.
Executive Director, Donna Hawley
P.O. Box 446
Nordman, ID 83848

Governing body of sled dog racing in the United States

International Weight Pulling Association
Mark Johnson, President
570 Timber Trail
Stevensville, MT 59870

National Animal Poison Control Center
900-680-0000
(charged $2.75/minute)
or 800-548-2423
Call the 800 number first and have a credit card ready; charge, $30 per case

Newfoundland Club of America
Roger Powell, NCA Land Work Secretary
5208 Olive Rd.
Raleigh, NC 27606
Can provide information on backpacking and carting, including plans for making packs, harness and carts

Responsible Dog Owners Association
13D, 73 Old Dublin Pike
Doylestown, PA 18901
215-249-1377
Nonprofit organization formed to educate the public on responsible dog ownership and promote the interests of dog owners

Identification

AKC Companion Animal Recovery
5580 Centerview Dr.
Suite 250
Raleigh, NC 27606-3394
800-252-7894
New AKC program for registering microchipped dogs; 24-hour lost dog line

I.D. Pet
74 Hoyt St.
Darien, CT 06820
800-243-9147
National tattoo registry organization

Instant ID Tag
Merion Station Mail Order Co.
P.O. Box 100
Merion Station, PA 19066
800-333-TAGS
Plastic tags to put on collar temporarily

Lost Paws
P.O. Box 781
Pleasant Hill, CA 94523
800-676-3157
Toll-free number for preregistered pets lost during travel (or at home)

National Dog Registry
P.O. Box 116
Woodstock, NY 12498
800-NDR-DOGS (800-637-3647)
National tattoo registry organization

National Pet Protection Network
United Pet Protection Services
7380 S. Eastern Ave.,
Suite 124-128
Las Vegas, NV 89123
Pet registration service

Pet Pocket ID
Diverse Designs Inc.
139 Harper St.
Louisville, CO 80027
800-786-9981
A nylon pocket with an ID card
inside, to slide onto collar

Pet Securities
Allred Enterprises Inc.
30 Kentwood Lane
Pisgah Forest, NC 28768
800-634-9651
Pet registration service

Tattoo-a-Pet
1625 Emmons Ave.
Brooklyn, NY 11235
800-828-8667
National tattoo registry
organization

Supplies

Adirondack Dog Sled
Manufacturing
Marshall Fish
Westport, NY 12993
518-962-4897

Aqua-Pet Life Vest
Windborne Products
114 Lincoln Dr.
Sausalito, CA 94965
415-331-3542

Black Ice Dog Sledding Equipment
3620 Yancy Ave.
New Germany, MN 55367
612-485-4825
Dog harnesses, sleds, booties, etc.

Dog Works
RR 3, Box 317, Curvin Circle
Stewartstown, PA 17363
800-787-2788
Dog harnesses, carts, backpacks

Hall Sleds and Rigs
Frank Hall
5875 McCrum Rd.
Jackson, MI 49201
517-782-1786

Happy Dog Car Seat
9268 N. Cottage Park Dr.
Mobile, AL 36695
334-633-3215
Car seat with safety harness for dogs
up to 25 pounds

Ikon Outfitters
7597 Latham Rd.
Lodi, WI 53555
608-592-4397
Canine recreational equipment

Lynchburg Hardware and
General Store
Lynchburg, TN 37352
615-759-4200
Dog wagons

K9 Cruiser bicycle leash
5151 Santa Fe L-2
San Diego, CA 92109
800-K9-CRUIS (800-592-7847)
Allows you to exercise dog alongside
bicycle

K-9 Sulkys
2406 N. Wood Ct.
Claremont, CA 91711
714-621-7511
Two-wheeled dog carts

Oasis Pet Products
2242 Davis Ct.
Hayward, CA 94545
Pet travel canteen

Odormute
Available in stores; combats skunk
odor on dogs and people

Pearson Towne & Country Carts
2260 N. Walnut St.
Muncie, IN 47305
317-289-2244
Two- and four-wheeled carts

Pet Care First Aid Kit
P.O. Box 59
Jericho, NY 11753
800-PET KITS (800-738-5487)
First-aid kit for dogs

PetProtect
P.O. Box 16115
Encino, CA 91416
800-564-7387
First-aid kit for dogs

Pooch Pouch
Barry Industries
P.O. Box 586311
Oceanside, CA 92056
800-850-8180
Fanny pack with poop scoop,
zippered pocket for keys, room for
ball, side pocket for treats

Retractable Flexi Tie-Out
Available from pet supply stores;
operates the same as a Flexi-Lead

Springer bike attachment
Allenfarm
1627 Union Street
Bangor, ME 04401
207-942-8758
Allows you to exercise dog alongside
bicycle

Wolf Packs
1679 Chalcedony
San Diego, CA 92109
Dog packs

Books and Other Publications

(Nearly all the books listed are
available through one toll-free phone
call to Direct Book Service, 800-
776-2665)

Guide to Backpacking with Your Dog
by Charlene G. LaBelle
Alpine Publications
P.O. Box 7027
Loveland, CO 80537
800-777-7257

Backpacking with Your Dog
by Richard Lerner, D.V.M.
Available from Direct Book Service

*Cart and Sled Dog Training; Building
a Training Cart; Novice Sled Dog
Training; Packing Dogs; Skijoring
with Dogs; Sled Building Plans*
by Raymond Thompson

Raymond Thompson Co.
15815 2nd Pl., W.
Lynwood, WA 98036

Carting Information Packet
Newfoundland Club of America
NCA Land Work Secretary,
Roger Powell
5208 Olive Rd.
Raleigh, NC 27606

Dog Driver:
A Guide for the Serious Musher
by Miki and Julie Collins
Alpine Publications
P.O. Box 7027
Loveland, CO 80537
800-777-7257

Dog Training (The Gentle Modern
Method)
by David Weston
Howell Book House
1633 Broadway
New York, NY 10019
800-428-5331

Dogwatching
by Desmond Morris
Crown Publishing Group
Random House
201 E. 50th St.
New York, NY 10022

Help! Quick Guide to First Aid
for Dogs
by Michelle Bamberger
Howell Book House
1633 Broadway
New York, NY 10019
800-428-5331

How to Raise a Puppy
You Can Live With
by Clarice Rutherford and
David H. Neil, MRCVS
Alpine Publications
P.O. Box 7027
Loveland, CO 80537
800-777-7257

How to Talk to Your Dog
by Jean Craighead George
Warner Books, Inc.
1271 Avenue of the Americas
New York, NY 10020

How to Teach a New Dog Old Tricks
by Ian Dunbar, Ph.D., MRCVS
James & Kenneth Publishers
2140 Shattuck Ave., #2406
Berkeley, CA 94704
510-658-8588

How to Teach Your Old Dog
New Tricks and *Communicating*
with Your Dog
by Ted Baer
Barrons Educational Series, Inc.
P.O. Box 8040
Hauppauge, NY 11788
800-645-3476

The Joy of Running Sled Dogs
by Noel Flanders
Alpine Publications
P.O. Box 7027
Loveland, CO 80537
800-777-7257

Mother Knows Best
by Carol Lea Benjamin
Howell Book House
1633 Broadway
New York, NY 10019
800-428-5331

Mush! The Beginners Manual of Sled Dog Training
Arner Publications
100 Bouck St.
Rome, NY 13440

*Newfoundland Draft Work:
A Guide for Training*
by Consie Powell
Consie and Roger Powell
Ottawa Newfoundlands
5208 Olive Rd.
Raleigh, NC 27606

*On the Road Again
with Man's Best Friend*
by Dawn and Robert Habgood
Five regions available:
New England, Mid-Atlantic,
Southeast, California and
Northwest
Howell Book House
1633 Broadway
New York, NY 10019
800-428-5331
Selective guides to bed and
breakfasts, inns, hotels and resorts
that welcome you and your pet

*Owner's Guide to Better Behavior
in Dogs and Cats*
by William Campbell
Alpine Publications
P.O. Box 7027

Loveland, CO 80537
800-777-7257

*The Pearsall Guide
to Successful Dog Training*
by Margaret E. Pearsall
Howell Book House
1633 Broadway
New York, NY 10019
800-428-5331

Poisonous Plants List
Rollins Publications
Attn: Plants
2615 Waugh
Suite 244
Houston, TX 77006

Sirius Puppy Training (video)
by Ian Dunbar, Ph.D., MRCVS
James & Kenneth Publishers
2140 Shattuck Ave., #2406
Berkeley, CA 94704
510-658-8588

Taking Your Dog Backpacking
by Alan Riley
Newfoundland Club of America
NCA Land Work Secretary,
Roger Powell
5208 Olive Rd.
Raleigh, NC 27606

Vacationing with Your Pet
by Eileen Barish
Pet Friendly Publications
P.O. Box 8459
Scottsdale, AZ 85252
800-496-2665
A directory of pet-friendly lodgings
across the country

Magazines

(Magazines offer a wealth of general care, behavior, and training information, and often articles on traveling with dogs.)

Dog Fancy
P.O. Box 53264
Boulder, CO 80322
303-666-8504

Dog World
P.O. Box 6500
Chicago, IL 60680
800-247-8080

Front and Finish
P.O. Box 333
Galesburg, IL 61402

Good Dog!
P.O.Box 10069
Austin, TX 78766
800-968-1738

Off-Lead
204 Lewis St.
Canastota, NY 13032
315-697-2749

Index